DONNA C

Let's Act Like
Rice

*Creating Health and Happiness
through Food and Everyday Life*

Illustrations by
EMMA SUDAK

Copyright © 2020 Donna Clifford.

All rights reserved. No part of this book may be reproduced, stored, or transmitted by any means—whether auditory, graphic, mechanical, or electronic—without written permission of the author, except in the case of brief excerpts used in critical articles and reviews. Unauthorized reproduction of any part of this work is illegal and is punishable by law.

Because of the dynamic nature of the Internet, any web addresses or links contained in this book may have changed since publication and may no longer be valid. The views expressed in this work are solely those of the author and do not necessarily reflect the views of the publisher, and the publisher hereby disclaims any responsibility for them.

Cover photograph by Getty Images

Scripture taken from the King James Version of the Bible.

ISBN: 978-1-7164-7335-7 (sc)
978-1-7164-7334-0 (e)

Library of Congress Control Number: 2020921480

Lulu Publishing Services rev. date: 12/17/2020

To my faithful husband who calls me darling and promised to never do me harm. He has kept that promise for thirty-five years and supports my every endeavor—regardless of how crazy or expensive it is. He's witnessed my transformation and I his, through this beautiful thing we call macrobiotics.

Contents

Foreword vii

Introduction xi

Chapter 1   Life Energy 1

Chapter 2   Make Grain Your Main 34

Chapter 3   Thy Own Biome 57

Chapter 4   Our Reflection 64

Chapter 5   Get Ready 68

Chapter 6   A Grain of Happiness 72

Chapter 7   Troupe Soup 116

Chapter 8   Team Beans 139

Chapter 9   The Festival of Vegetables 160

Chapter 10 The Blessings of Dressings 192

Chapter 11 In a Pickle Now! 206

Chapter 12 The Notion That the Potion Is in the Ocean 212

Chapter 13 Sweet Treats 227

Chapter 14 Life without Breath 248

Chapter 15 The Invisible Invaders 255

Chapter 16 You Will Know You're Acting Like Rice When 263

Chapter 17 It Took a Village 265

References 271

Index 274

Foreword

We have a special relationship with plants. They provide us with food, either by eating them directly, or indirectly, by eating the animals that eat them. They also provide us with the oxygen we breathe. Not only are plants a source of food; they are also a source of medicine and healing.

Plants and humans, who are members of the animal world, are at the opposite end of the biological spectrum. The word "medicine" is derived from the Latin "medi," or "middle," hence words such as "median" and "medium." The suffix "cine" is from the ancient Greek "kineo," which means "to move." Medicine is thus the art of moving toward the middle or away from the extremes. Biologically this means to rely primarily on plants both as food and as medicine. In so doing, we move toward our opposite—and thus toward the middle.

Hippocrates, the founder of modern medicine, famously said, "Let thy food be thy medicine and thy medicine be thy food." Thus, if we adhere to Hippocrates's dictum, we base our diet on plant foods and utilize common plant foods as our first line of remedy for illness. Plants are the foundation of Traditional Chinese Medicine. They are the foundation of Ayurveda, the healing systems of ancient Greece, traditional Arabic medicine, and of all the world's great healing systems.

The founder of Chinese medicine, Shennong, or the "divine farmer," is said to have experimented with hundreds of medicinal plants to determine which ones were effective in treating disease. The first text of herbal medicine, the *Shennong Ben Cao Jing*, was compiled during the first century BC and classified 365 herbs and medicinal plants. Chinese medicine was introduced into Japan around the sixth century AD and again, focused on the use of herbs and medicinal plants. These practices became known as *Kanpo*, or "Chinese medicine," and are used today throughout Asia. They are growing in popularity in Europe, America, and throughout the world.

Using common foods to heal and restore balance captures the essence of Hippocrates's dictum to let food be our medicine and medicine be our food. Every day, we adjust to our changing environments. We eat different foods, exercise and move differently, and sleep in unique patterns. Our interactions with people change, as do the stresses, or lack of stresses, we face.

Weather is a huge environmental influence. When we adapt successfully, health and vitality are the result. When we are slow or unable to adapt, the result is a variety of adjustments, which serve to reset our condition in harmony with external changes. These resets take the form of a variety of conditions, some superficial and short-lived, others deeper and longer-lasting. Food is the means by which we readjust or recalibrate our condition on a day-to-day basis to maintain health and balance or to restore health and balance if lost. That is the meaning of "food as medicine."

In this book, Donna Clifford, a veteran of decades of holistic and modern medicine, explains the role of food in health and healing. She updates Hippocrates for modern readers, and brings him into the twenty-first century. Roll over, Hippocrates and Shennong—Donna has now arrived on the scene.

Here you will survey the scope of nutritional and energetic healing. Donna emphasizes a plant-based diet as the foundation for health and healing, especially the importance of brown rice and other whole grains. From that base, she expands on other categories of foods that make up a complete, plant-based, whole foods diet. Donna's approach is holistic—she presents the latest nutritional findings supporting a plant-based diet, and she also explains the centuries-old energetic approach that also supports this way of eating.

With her extensive professional background, Donna is at the cutting edge of a new medicine, a medicine for humanity. The medicine of humanity can prevent and heal individual sicknesses. It can also advance the movement toward a healthy and peaceful world. It is my hope that you will use this book as a practical guide to healthful living. In addition, my hope is that society at large will take Donna's message to heart in its quest for a healthy, peaceful, and sustainable future.

—Edward Esko
Founder, International Macrobiotic Institute
Author, *Macrobiotic Nutrition*

Introduction

Many before me have promised the secret of happiness by using their product. I am here with nothing to sell, only the hope that you will tap into your own healing energy, which is yours, and only yours, and find happiness on a magnitude that is unimaginable. Miracles happen every day when you live your authentic life. I know this because I have worked with people of all races, ages, nationalities, sexes, with an array of sicknesses and challenges, and found one common thread. When a person eats human food, aligns their energy, and explores their inner landscape, abundance follows, health returns, dreams come true, and the impossible becomes possible. It never fails.

It took almost a lifetime to have these secrets revealed to me. You see, I was born with irreversible birth defects. I may look normal on the outside, but I am extremely sick on the inside, making my struggles in life difficult for others to see. Because no one knew of my challenges, I had to work harder to be equal. My life search was to find a cure for what is incurable. Through my healing work, I did. Now I share what I have learned for others to cure their incurables.

Healing encompasses all levels of a human being. We begin a journey on the physical level by seeing a health care professional. Because we are not only a body, our emotions and spiritual destiny are interwoven through our flesh as consciousness. If we are open to seeing our true selves, we continue a healing journey of self-discovery and realize our lives on a meaningful level. The self-realization fills our capacity and completes our lives.

Here are examples of realization.

I worked with a loved one who as a child wanted to please his parent. We discovered this while he began a grain-based diet and chakra alignment (described later in book). In every attempt, the parent did not recognize the child's achievements and criticized his effort. The child tried harder and harder to gain parental acceptance and love. Over the years, he did not recognize his self-worth and developed unhealthy relationships. The child, now an adult, accomplished a major life goal. The parent looks the other way and praises the work of a sibling instead. The child says to himself in an aha moment, "Nothing I do will ever be good enough for you." It hits like a lightning bolt. The realization is awareness that is incorporated to every cell of his being. Suddenly his health improves, he walks with pride, and he no longer believes he is not lovable. He knew this information all along, but now he is self-realized. He has embodied the words.

The same is true for a woman who came to me with many health conditions requiring several medications. We learned through energy work that she believed she was ugly, and her chakras aligned to that thought. She was not thin enough or tall enough, and she didn't match the models in the media. Her inner self revealed her beauty to her in a session of chakra alignment. She burst into tears and repeated, "I really am pretty." Her life changed dramatically that day and she found her value.

My lifelong friend Cathy shared her experience with me after her mom died. "A treasure is not something you find—it's what you come to realize you have." I love meditating on that thought.

Self-realization can be attained through meditation practices or life lessons. It is the realization of one's self and the truth of one's existence that is liberating knowledge of the true self at a time the spirit is ready to listen.

It is our realization that engrains learning into our belief systems, our beliefs program our chakras, and our chakras program our physical and emotional lives. This is what I wish to share with you. Health and happiness are bound together. It is difficult to have one without the other. Health does not come from a pill or a shot. It comes from the soil, the earth, and the cosmos. I believe that healing is an evolutionary process that brings us further into our destined lives. This book is written for those who are thirsty for the knowledge to change how they feel, hungry with anticipation to try new ideas, crave the ability to participate in their own lives, and have an appetite for happiness.

I wrote this book because I believe that we do not appreciate why we are sick, why we suffer, and why we eat and behave like we do. Our understanding is limited, and the answers seem to be outside of us. How many of us perceive our suffering to be caused by us? Isn't it always someone else's fault or a punishment from God? At one time, I did not know either. This book will explain how we create our own health and destiny. Then you will know. *Let us Act Like Rice* will give you the foundation to change. Are you ready for change?

Why rice? The roots of individual rice seeds grow underground and entwine with other rice seed roots like a woven cloth to strengthen the whole paddy. Human behavior mimics the rice's behavior when the constituents of rice are eaten. Families who eat rice together meld together and have the capability of melding with others to strengthen the whole. Can you envision a world of oneness? What a world it would be.

Grain eating is how happy humans evolved into the present day until modern life led us astray. We can now enter a grocery store twelve months a year and buy food from around the world. We are very confused about what to eat. We are so confused, in fact, that at any given gathering, you will find people on many different diets, including paleo, keto, macro, vegan, raw, and fasting.

Are we arrogant enough to believe that we can eat and live however we want without any consequences to our health and happiness? Yes, we are because we do. When we do not acknowledge and follow the laws of nature, nature will win in the end. The cost is our personal health, our family's health, the health of our schools, communities, and the health of the planet. When we eat seasonally, locally, and naturally, humanness comes forward, and we feel human and behave humanly. The energy that is imparted when eating rice and all grains is one of peace and calmness, which transfers to peaceful individuals, families, communities, countries, and even worlds. When we leave the natural world of grain eating and eat unnatural food, our thoughts will follow an unnatural path. It is natural for us to live in groups or families and work as teams. It is unnatural to feel isolated and unworthy. Throughout my practice of healing with others, I find a strong correlation between how natural the diet is and the intensity of the feelings of not being good enough. The more natural the diet, the more value and esteem we have.

Are we developing stronger as a species? We have modern technology and science and require more education for entry-level jobs, yet our civilization is degenerating. We see this in education, health care, politics, and social norms. We do not behave with dignity or manners anymore. Just turn on the TV and see the violence, greed, and materialism in epic proportions.

As the diet degrades from nature, the mind and body degrade from nature. It may sound too simple, but it is undeniable. We all suffer in one way or another, and I see this every day as a nurse. Much of our suffering can be under our control and be eliminated, bringing us joy like dancing in the sunny rice field. Cancer and disability affect the patient, the family, and the health care and educational systems, and the suffering extends into the community. Our hospitals and community services are stressed while working on tight budgets. But rice, you see, grows in a sunny field, blowing in the wind, and is happy. Let us find that happiness and act like rice.

What makes me qualified to assess your life? Why should you listen to me? Here is a bit of my story. It was 1982, upon graduating North Shore Community College's nursing program, that I carried a wealth of book knowledge into my new career as an adult. I felt like a big shot as an identified professional wearing a white cap, black stripe, and a pin. It did not take long to discover that it was only the beginning of learning this new environment called nursing. What I did not know at the time was how life-changing learning is and how it would carve my way into the world.

I soon transitioned into an ICU position and learned very quickly how important I was. Perhaps a class on humility would have served me. I felt empowered to have control over a human life based on knowledge that I had learned in school. My experiences in this role provided me pride enough to last ten years in this setting. The hectic life of an ICU nurse caring for critically ill patients clearly showed me the fragility of life and the adaptability of the human spirit. Life is fragile. It can change in a split second. It is there that I learned the seriousness of illness and how my judgments and decisions will impact a patient and their family. This lesson came with maturity a decade after leaving the job.

The next challenge for me was to work in our fast-paced telemetry unit. Over the next eighteen years, I thought I learned all there was to learn about the heart and the protocols that align with health. I had the opportunity to float to other units in times of nursing demands. This led to me to view patient care in the areas of interventional radiology, labor and delivery, infusion, IV therapy, and endoscopy.

The repetition of caring for patients with cancer in the Oncology Unit was the beginning of my next chapter of learning. I noticed similarities in the stories that patients would tell me. Before the dawning of the computer, nurses had time to talk with patients. I noticed that cancer patients spoke of stories relating to helplessness. Patients with cardiopulmonary issues reflected upon their grief and loneliness. Patients receiving dialysis spoke of fear, and those with liver and gallbladder illnesses felt rage. It is interesting that I also noted an aroma to each disease category. Because my colleagues did not have this observation, I decided to keep it to myself and continue to observe. I didn't know at the time that I was learning about the human energy field. This knowledge would lay the foundation for my future work in healing.

Massage school was entered with the expectation of ramping up my resume. This superficial thinking was quickly shaken when my training included deep reflection, healing of issues, which I did not know I had, and the responsibility of creating my destiny. After twelve hundred hours of training, the girl who walked into the Polarity Realization Institute was not the same girl who left. I saw the world in terms of energy, chakras, color, sound, and vibration.

I also began a personal transformation and no longer drank alcohol, smoked cigarettes, or ate meat or sugar. I had always enjoyed coffee and cigarettes and never intended to relinquish them. These behaviors were part of my nursing culture and kept me socially accepted, but as I healed, these energies no longer served me—and eliminating them was effortless.

As I learned new energy work, my vibration raised, and I did not resonate with the vibration of my prior choices. At the time, I was only interested in building my resume and not a lifestyle change. The universe was guiding me in this direction without my awareness. I could not yet see the bigger picture. Changing my diet and lifestyle made me seem weird to others, and I was seen as socially awkward. People looked at me with a raised eyebrow because I did not eat the birthday cake or have a purse full of over-the-counter medications to share. After all, I was a nurse! I was and still am remarkably comfortable with my weirdness. I walked through a door of healing, and there was no going back into unconsciousness. When a door of learning opens, a thousand other doors open in parallel, showing us how much we do not know. We must learn to follow our higher guidance.

Polarity therapy training was a necessity if I was going to continue an energetic practice. In another 650 hours, I became a registered polarity practitioner. I began to shape my destiny. I opened and operated New Aura, a holistic healing center with two locations in Salem, Massachusetts.

I saw and worked on thousands of people in need of healing. The word *patient* had now been replaced with *loved one* since that was what was doing the healing.

Through the work of polarity therapy, I was privileged to be a part of spectacular events in other people's lives. I witnessed addicts recover, cancers disappear, emotional recoveries of anxiety and depression, and chronic pain and degenerative disease become a memory. Each loved one had self-realizations and an understanding of their disease process and their role in the making of their suffering. When brought to awareness, energy changes health quickly. When we hear our universal signals, our clarity and intuition become stronger, allowing us to have knowledge and confidence to create the life we wish. The signals get stronger and stronger until you take notice. This may come in some type of dramatic life event like sickness or a major accident. Staying in touch with our inner world and our guidance prevents this dramatic occurrence. We learn to hear the subtle signals.

Everything about my life changed. Nothing seemed hopeless or impossible. From the texts, I learned the anatomy of the chakras and aura, and in practice, I entrained with it with all my senses. One day at school, we were learning about distance healing where the loved one and the practitioner are in different locations. The practitioner calls forth the loved one's energy through a holographic effect and clears energetic stagnation with the use of clear quartz crystals.

When it was my turn to be the loved one, I went into a private room while another student worked on me from a distance. I lay on the carpeted floor with my eyes closed, and for a few minutes, I thought, *This is ridiculous. This would never be accepted in the medical field.* However, I kept an open mind and enjoyed the silence. Within minutes, I had a very real event. I began to reexperience the smell of the anesthetic ether I had as a child during surgery. I felt smothered, helpless, and terrified just as I did when I was four years old. The smell got stronger and stronger until I could hardly breathe.

Just as I was going to get up and leave, a bright light came into the room and filled me with overwhelming love, gratitude, and happiness. The trauma that I had unconsciously carried with me had been cleared and replaced with something much higher. I learned to never fear sickness because in it is beautiful healing. By the way, the room had no windows! There are many unconscious ways we show who we are on a deep level. When you examine someone's sublime energy form, the true nature is revealed. Since this experience, I have entered a partnership in weekly distance healing with a man who lives in Japan.

What did I do with this training? Doctors I worked with wanted me to work with their patients and were instrumental in helping me obtain a home license to see their patients. Amazing things happened in my little home office. I worked with people with every conceivable health condition. Hundreds passed through my doors, resulting in new realizations. I watched and documented as patients' medication doses were decreased and eventually discontinued. I witnessed chronic pain melt into thin air; lung disease, diabetes, Crohn's disease, hepatitis, infertility—you name it, it changed! It has been my greatest honor and a privilege to be a part of someone's true healing journey.

We are copulations of organized energy. Knowing this allows us to understand our challenges, struggles, and purpose. We reflect our energy in each other, leading us to believe it is the other person's fault or character. That was a good eye-opener for me. I started practicing—and I still practice—energy principles in every aspect of my life. We must contemplate our hardships to find the answer that leads to happiness. This occurs on the spiritual and energetic levels first, and then it manifests into the physical realm of reality.

The frosting on this cake began as I entered a lifelong study of macrobiotics. I heard references to the terms yin and yang in polarity school and found them intriguing. Who knew that the leading macrobiotic school in the world was right here in my backyard in Beckett, Massachusetts? Through my training, I thought I was learning about health and disease, but I was learning about life. Can that go on a resume?

I learned the most powerful concept of science and medicine is called yin and yang. They are energetic terms of complementary opposites that occur everywhere in the natural world. It is as complex as it is simple. I attended classes and completed all the training that they offered. It was the most fascinating material I had ever learned because it could be applied to all aspects of life.

Again, I witnessed cures for the incurable. Cancers and degenerative diseases were no longer a threat if macrobiotic principles were followed. People came to the Kushi Institute, broken and weak, and they left their wheelchairs and crutches behind as they left the institute, strong and vital. I am still in awe at the level of healing that happened at a school! It was not a hospital or clinic, and health insurance had no impact on the treatment. I met doctors and healers from around the world at the Kushi Institute. They took macrobiotic knowledge back to their home practices to their patients. Lucky patients.

Over the years, I have become certified and/or licensed in massage therapy, La-stone therapy, Shiatsu, Foot reflexology, body-centered meditation, polarity therapy, macrobiotic counseling, Ayurveda, and food-safety management. Like building blocks of healing, I have constructed a view of health that explains why we suffer and do not live the lives we desire. We are doing it all wrong! Focus, money, attention, and other resources are moving in the opposite direction than health. Every scientific advance moves us further into a modern life that affects our ability to adapt to our environments and stay well.

At the KI, I witnessed the most intriguing treatments and recoveries of cancer, and for some time, I was not sure if these teachers, healers, and gurus were brilliant or crazy. As I absorbed all this information and allowed the learning to transform me, the answer became clear. My health changed, and I became ridiculously happy. Some healing hits you like a slap in the face, and other healing needs to marinate.

Over time, the tools taught me to not be fearful, have patience, be forgiving, and look deep within myself for change. It is exceedingly difficult to have a fault and change it. People spend a lifetime in therapy or rehab trying to change behavior. It can be very frightening to connect to one's suffering or explore one's trauma, but it can be done in a beautiful and enlightening way. Healing is a journey for which the outcome is not known. The beliefs that formed our energy patterns—and thus our bodies—can change quickly or slowly. When the belief changes, the energy aligns to that belief, and then the body follows the pattern.

I conducted in a six-month study at Union Hospital in Lynn, Massachusetts, utilizing crystal bodywork and polarity therapy. With the support of a cardiologist, the study was approved by an institutional review board (IRB). A doctor's order was necessary for the patient to be in the study, and I worked with selected patients in unprofitable diagnosis-related groups. A DRG is a diagnosis-related group that standardizes payments made to hospitals. I educated all medical staff in workshops to familiarize them with the work. If they were not aware of its value, why would they order it? I also gave free sessions to show the effects of energy work.

The results were in the hospital's favor. Length of stay was shortened, less postoperative pain medicine was required, and patients' anxiety was lessened. Patients and their families recorded that strained relationships between them had been restored. Wow! I would like to see a pharmaceutical do that! My findings were published in *Energy News*, a polarity therapy journal. The energy people were not excited about work being done in a hospital setting, and the medical people were not interested in a service that could not be submitted for reimbursement. Ironically, my medical colleagues do not appreciate that I am holistic, and my holistic colleagues are not impressed that I am a nurse.

My teachers have educated me in the best of science, energy, and macrobiotics, giving me the understanding of health and illness in a unique way. In fact, I find this subject so exciting that I have read nearly every book about macrobiotics. I have searched old volumes and found original Japanese writings translated to English. It has become my work, my hobby, and my obsession. I hope this inspires you in your journey of healing.

In *Men in Black,* Wil Smith was a federal agent with the knowledge of aliens on the planet. He was privileged to have access to information that could change the world, but he was forbidden to reveal this information because it could very well create a panic. No one would believe that insects were living in human bodies. To understand the human energy field and macrobiotics is to be a man in black because the knowledge is life changing to all of humanity. Grain eating allows you a clear vision of the world and the destiny of humanity, but it's kept secret because no one would believe it. If you want to be a man in black too, keep reading.

There is an expanding body of evidence validating that a plant-based diet reverses degenerative diseases and has been shown to be essential in its prevention. Macrobiotics goes a step further than a plant-based diet.

Based in the ancient wisdom of yin and yang, eating macrobiotically creates health, balance, and happiness. The balance is reflected in the physical body, emotional stability, and the connectedness to others. These words sound cliché, but the feeling is of oneness and belonging to a greater whole.

Our bodies have an internal wisdom that knows exactly how to heal itself. For instance, when we cut ourselves, we bleed to cleanse the wound. A clot forms over the wound as a scab to prevent bleeding to death. The scab is a natural Band-Aid to prevent bacteria from entering through broken skin. The wound edges adhere together, and skin cells proliferate to seal the cut. Zebra cells do not form here. Liver cells do not form here. Human skin cells form here because the body is programmed to repair itself. When given the correct conditions, the body has an astounding ability to kill cancer cells, repair organs, communicate happiness, and reverse degeneration. We just need to get out of the way!

People ask me exactly what this diet is. Here is my response. Humans have always lived in harmony with the laws of nature. We have always had a relationship with the foods we ate. Families grew their food long before takeout was popular. They planted and watched the daily changes in their food as it grew. Humans knew their food, and the food knew the humans.

Living within nature, sickness was cured naturally. Our grandmothers all knew to head to the kitchen at the first sign of a cold. Humans have come a long way from instinctual knowledge. We now have super-mega grocery stores, fake meat, fake food, factory-farmed animals, fast furniture, indoor heating and air-conditioning, and a slew of pesticides, chemicals, plastics, and electromagnetic fields.

In many ways, humans have lost their connection to nature. We live and work in modern offices and homes. Even our modern appliances take us away from nature by doing the tasks for us. If we use a smart appliance, we no longer have to even press the button. Our feet do not connect to the earth while wearing modern footwear, especially high heels. We may incidentally walk barefoot outdoors in summertime over concrete or chemically treated grass. At any given moment, would we know the incoming tide or what is growing locally? We are eating more and sleeping less.

The modern lifestyle has brought us to where we are today. Sick! Like ick in a fish tank, we are living among our own pollution and suffering with cancer, diabetes, and dementia. Almost every disease classification is epidemic. In every culture, it was the poor who ate beans and grain and the rich who ate animal-based foods. While the wealthy suffered degenerative diseases, the plant eaters were the laborers due to their strong physical fitness. For them, meat was eaten in small amounts only to flavor a dish. Modern humans eat animals three times a day and in large quantities. Today, we all live like kings.

Macrobiotics is the path back to natural living in a modern world. Preparing whole foods with simple ingredients balances the stress of everyday life and cleanses and regenerates our bodies and minds. Whole foods relax the internal organs, creating a calmness about oneself. You may not be able to control outside stressors, but your reactions can be from a state of balance and groundedness. This is the effect of a macrobiotic diet.

Macrobiotic foods clear, repair, and align our sublime energies, such as our meridians, chakras, and auras. Alignment comes naturally. The body cleanses itself, aligns its energies, and rejoins its family of origin—the infinite universe—simply by eating. Many have never felt this state of being as normalcy, which brings varying degrees of physical and emotional fatigue. Those lower feelings will transform into higher human feelings of joy, vibrancy, and the connection to something real.

The macrobiotic diet is a balance of yin and yang, contraction and expansion, acid and alkaline, and the rhythms of nature. Eating is a mechanism to connect you to your food. Food becomes you! That is amazing. Just think that at one time your bones and organs were once on your plate!

Eating grains and vegetables connects you to the glory of the world that is here for all of us to enjoy—through nature. It creates higher thinking that brings us a natural resilience and allows us to face adversity head-on with strength and personal power. Eating in a macrobiotic manner also connects us to each other. This builds strong families and communities. Imagine if everyone ate this way. We would experience the promise of the one peaceful world that has been spoken by my teacher, Michio Kushi.

Lillian Clifford age 9

Let's Act Like Rice is a message and a plan to create the life you have been dreaming of. We will always have stress and responsibilities—I can't offer magic to change that—but I can show you the magic that begins with eating grains, and you can decide how you want to use it. I wrote this book to stop the suffering that we have control over.

How many parents watch their children suffer with sickness or addiction? How many of us suffer as we watch our parents age and decline? How many suffer, wishing to live a better life but feeling trapped? I have watched people and their families suffer every day in hospitals. We do not need to bear strokes, heart disease, dementia, and cancer. This is suffering that we have control over. We all suffer. In fact, our growth reflects the outcome of our suffering.

One does not experience spiritual growth through joy. Life's hard lessons teach us to be resilient. Life does not need to be faced with needless complications. If you follow the suggestions in the following pages, you will face your stress with a relaxed and joyful attitude and find the meaning behind the stress. Everything happens for a reason. Right? Do we ever know what the reason is? When we listen to our clues from our inner knowing, the truth will always be revealed. Eating grains will erase the static in our heads so that we can enter our inner thoughts without distraction. We will find that we can handle our hardships with calmness and focus.

The words in this book may help us remember who we are on all levels: physical, emotional, and spiritual. Come along for the journey. Each of us has a vision of our perfect life. This book will help you find your connection to the abundance of joy that is yours and identify the purpose of your existence. Let's act like rice.

Chapter 1

Life Energy

Under the physical flesh lies the spirit of the human being. It is woven through our cells, memories, and aspirations. Let us call it the spark of life that flows throughout our bodies and minds. It has been referred to as prana, chi, ki, or life force.

All natural living things have a life force. Consider it as your nine-volt battery. A flower that is supple and radiant with color has a strong life force. A flower that is wilted and dry is losing its life force. We, like flowers, thrive when our life forces are strong and wither when they are not. Our life force is made of invisible sublime energy that moves through our bodies and pulsates with the rhythm of our breaths. Like the ebb and flow of the tide, life force expands and contracts in waves. Because I am an endoscopy nurse, I see it like peristalsis (Webster, ND).

We are all compilations of energy. Energy is simply the essence of our basic existence. It is the life force that flows through all natural things. It is the spirit of the breath within the breath. Our life force is the blueprint of our physical, emotional, and spiritual form. It surges life throughout our bodies. Our life force is simply the force of life. Our lives are more valuable than money. What price would you put on being fully alive?

My assignment one day in ICU was to care for two patients. One patient had been in a motorcycle accident, and the X-ray showed that his helmet separated the brain from the spinal column and endogenously decapitated him. He was on life support equipment and had no brain waves.

The other patient was also on life support because he was in congestive heart failure and was very much alive. What was the difference between these two patients? They both had heartbeats. They both had a normal temperature of 98.6 Fahrenheit. They both had circulation, pulses, urine output, etc. One of the patients would go home—and one would not. The patient in the accident had no circulating life force, meaning his spirit had left, most likely at the time of impact. His physical body was kept alive, but his essence or life force was gone.

Keeping life force strong takes effort. Draining life force takes effort as well. The spark of life that whirls within us is vibrational. It has both high and low frequencies. Vibration resonates with other vibrations in the same way as striking the middle C on a piano; all other C octaves will resonate with that vibration. That is how we resonate with our environments. Our environment is comprised of the people in our lives, the people we see in the media, and the plants, the animals, and the trees in our local area. We resonate with the foods we eat and the vibrations that we take in our mouths, ears, eyes, noses, and thoughts.

There may not be science to back this up yet, but in healing, this we know to be true:

- We are vibrational and resonate with vibrations around us.
- Each of us is special.
- Each of us came to earth for a specific reason.
- We are all made from love and truth.
- No one is different.
- We are all the same.
- We are bundles of light and love arranged in human form.
- Our consciousness is endless.
- We are all connected as one energy.
- We are not separate from holiness or each other.

When we allow blocks in our chakra patterns, we shut off light and love, which blocks the presence of God. Clearing our blocks brings light to dark places within us and gives rise to self-love and love for each other:

- I am part of you, and you are part of me.

- We are connected in many ways. The breath I breathed today will be the breath you breathe tomorrow and vice versa.
- We are never alone. Loneliness is impossible because we are part of oneness and are all sentient beings.
- We are connected through higher consciousness.
- We are connected through nature when we eat nature.
- We are connected through compassion and empathy. You feel my pain because you are part of me and vice versa.
- We came to this earth from a universal source of love some may know as God. We are all a part of the love that brought us here.
- Joy has never been lost to us. We disconnect from it; it does not disconnect from us.
- Joy is a natural state and will radiate outward to touch others.

You are an expression of love. Yes! You! We may have forgotten this truth because life has a way of distracting us from our true lives. The stress of financial strains, work and family demands, and intense schedules pulls us into our thoughts, and we leave the presence of our bodies. We are busy making money, working long hours, caring for children and parents, fighting social injustice, caring for our homes, cars, and prized possessions, and surviving divorce, school, trauma, abuse, and chronic illness. It is stress, stress, stress, stress, stress!

When we live in urgent chaos, attending to what is critical, we forget what is important. You may be reciting the many ways that this does not apply to you, but it does. It does not matter if you suffer from a disease that you believe has nothing to do with diet or lifestyle. It does not matter if you follow a particular religion or have none at all. It does not matter if you feel unworthy. It does not matter if you are dying of cancer. It does not matter how old you are. It does not matter if your doctor or counselor told you something otherwise. It does not matter if you don't believe in healing. It just does not matter.

Every one of us can change our health in some proportion, have joy and love with extraordinarily little effort, and act like rice. Let go of your distractions and live for your purpose. Understanding energy is the way of self-realization. Becoming connected to universal energy is a state of happiness that leaves a grin on your face that makes people think you're up to something.

To access your life force, we will require a quick lesson in anatomical energetic anatomy.

Crown Chakra	Spirituality
Third Eye Chakra	Intuition
Throat Chakra	Communication
Heart Chakra	Love, Gratitude
Solar Plexus Chakra	Will
Sacral Chakra	Sexuality, Creativity
Root Chakra	Basic Trust

We incarnate into our human bodies through an invisible energetic spiral on the top of the head. You may see this spiral in your hair pattern. All of life has a spiraling pattern. The energy from the heavens, which is called heaven's force, pushes energy down into a central channel that runs along the spine, which is called the shushumna. Energy from the earth, called earth's force, rises through the central channel. Growing up, I always heard people say, "Stand up straight." Maybe our prior generations knew about the shushumna. Where these two energies clash into each other creates a cone-shaped magnetic vortex of energy along the central channel and extending through the front and back of the body.

These areas are called chakras—an intersection of energetic pathways. They are highly charged wheels of light and consciousness. Chakras are made from the vibration of heaven and earth. Each chakra has an in valve and an out valve, and life force, or prana, flows freely through the chakra system, allowing us to manifest physically, emotionally, and spiritually in the world. That means that it is through the chakras that we incarnate our soul or spirit into our bodies.

Each of us possesses 114 chakras in our physical and ethereal bodies. There are seven main chakras that align our central core. Starting at the head, they are:

- the crown chakra
- the third eye chakra
- the throat chakra
- the heart chakra
- the solar plexus chakra
- the sacral chakra
- the base chakra

Energy becomes denser from the crown to the base. The upper chakras in general are more spiritual in nature, and the lower chakras keep us grounded on earth. The taking in of physical food nourishes the lower chakras, and taking in higher vibrations like music, prayer, or love, nourishes the upper chakras. Upon death, the lighter energy (spirit) ascends, and the denser vibration (body) returns to the earth.

The two magnetic forces supporting the structure of the chakras are referred to as the Ida and Pingala. They are the cleansing function of the energy system.

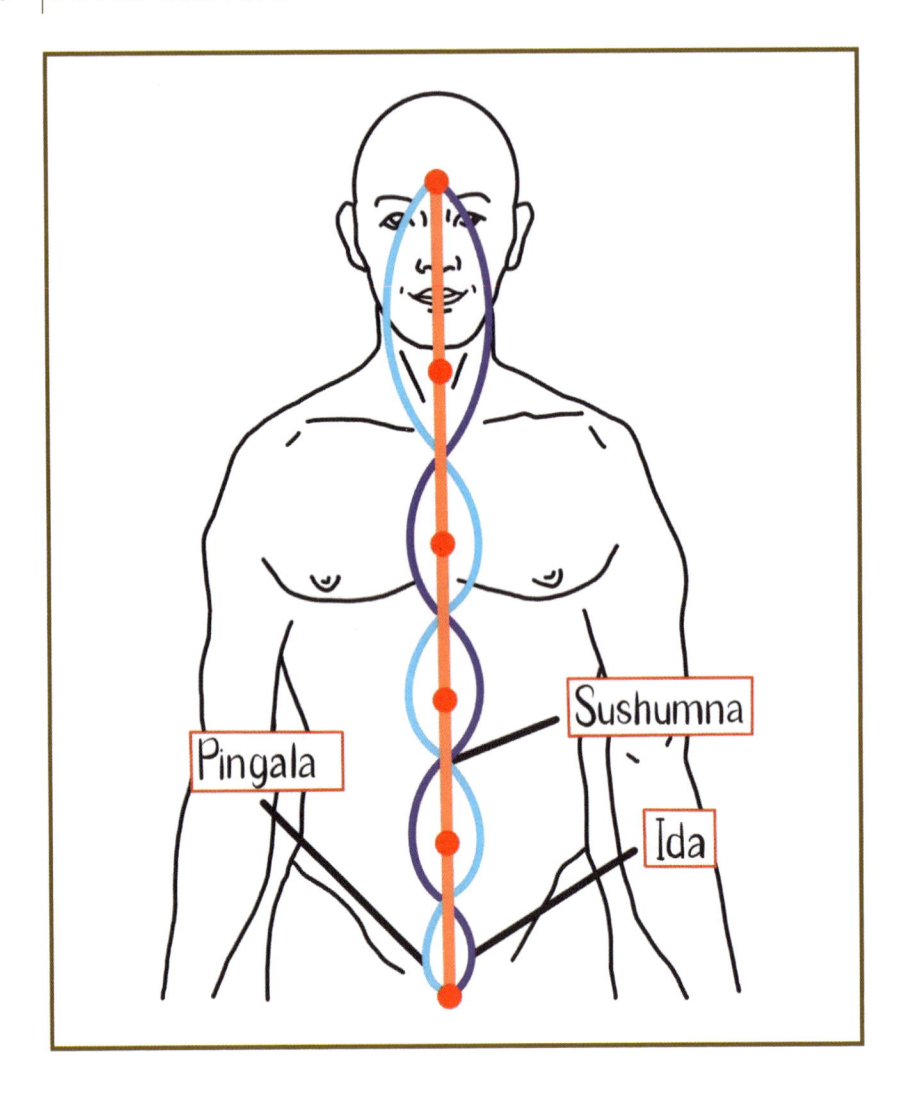

The chakra system allows us to form beliefs around ourselves by observing our environments. Our chakras are like mirrors, and we see our reflections though others. If there is a character trait or quality that you love about someone, it reflects yourself. The same is true if someone presses your button and brings up your pet peeve. Yup, it's a reflection of yourself. It means you have that quality inside of you, which you are unconscious about. It takes time and a certain amount of maturity to see our negative reflections on others. After you deny that you are anything like the offender, reflect on how you are like that person and create change.

We may find the offensive behavior in another area of Ida and Pingala. Ask a trusted friend for their truthful opinion. For example, I get really perturbed when circling the parking lot for a parking space and someone enters the circle and gets the space right in front of me. Ugh! When I sit and reflect, I find that I do the same thing in line at the grocery store. I must infuriate others.

It's okay to see your imperfections. My biggest pet peeve is the wasting of electricity or water. I am always shutting off lights at work. Why do so many lights need to be on when no one is in the room? So then, I reflect on what I waste in other areas of my life. Money? Time? Kindness? This is how we learn through the chakra mirror. They are learning tools for transformation. It takes practice and patience.

Begin to explore your chakra mirror by shutting off the world for a moment and sitting quietly. Take a few moments to breathe. Close your eyes and think about a memory or problem in your life, something that really grabs you and brings up emotion.

Notice where you feel it in your body. Without judgment or thought, simply sit with the emotion and watch. As though you are the observer, allow this emotion to transform into something else. Just let it happen without your control. What is the basic message? Trust, love, patience? Let the energies settle, and you may have a new awareness about this situation when you least expect it.

We can use our sublime energies to manifest our desires in life if we are willing to investigate our chakra mirrors. When the problem changes or an answer presents itself, you will know your inner voice.

Through the practice of both prayer and meditation, we enter the inner realm of healing. Prayer is the act of speaking. Most of us know how to pray and ask for something to change our lives, but meditation requires stillness and quiet because it is the act of listening. How many of us can sit quietly and listen? Channeling energy is a form of even deeper listening. Listen to your own inner voice, enter the journey of healing, and honor the self. Where the mind goes, energy flows.

The mind helps us to manage stress with coping mechanisms such as denial, repression, and projection. They keep us safe from the truth that hurts and prevent us from living our truth by not feeling the truth. Leland Val Van Dewall said, "The degree in which a person can grow is directly proportionate to the amount of truth he can accept about himself without running away."

Our unconscious coping mechanisms prevent us from going within to see our honest reality. We must go beyond the mind and beyond our coping mechanisms. The more outside of ourselves we are, the more anxious we become. We find safety and calmness in the truth that lives inside all of us. Bringing awareness to an unconscious place within us begins the healing journey. Healing is like peeling an onion, revealing each layer of ourselves. While the layers are peeled, the spirit opens gently like a lotus blossom. You cannot change what's going on around you until you change what's going on within you. If you do not go within, you will go without.

Our chakras can become blocked by negative energy that is unable to release from the body. If a block in a chakra intensifies, it blocks other chakras in a reflex fashion. Negative energy gets stuck within us from traumatic life experiences, emotional challenges, and poor eating. Because energy is magnetic, the blockage will attract more of itself to itself. For instance, someone who sees themselves as worthless will attract many opportunities into their life to prove that it is true. It is a self-fulfilling prophecy. The idea of being worthless is planted in their sublime energies and is realized.

When energy is realized, the entire body believes the thought. This is a second chakra blockage. The block will attract more negative energy to it. The blocked chakra can affect bowel function, fertility, menstruation, or pelvic disorders. The thyroid will not produce adequate amounts of thyroxine because, after all, the person is not worth it. The adrenals will slow down hormone production to fulfill the thought of unworthiness. By now, the person feels exhausted and unable to manage daily stress. In turn they consume coffee, alcohol, or sugar to feel better. Now more energetic blocks occur, and the system begins to break down, resulting in systemic disease and emotional collapse. Our chakras align to our thoughts. When we are aligned to glory and love, that is what flows through us. When we align to our distractions of life, that is what flows within us. Which will prevail? (R., 2016)

The same is true if someone believes that life is rich. The chakras align to that thought, and each chakra's corresponding endocrine gland will be charged for optimal performance. The magnetic vibration of happiness will attract more happiness to it, fulfilling the prophecy. Opportunities in life will arise to confirm the fact that they are happy. Have you ever seen how some people always have good things happen to them and others seem to always attract crap? Well, it is the condition of the chakra system attracting more of itself. There is a direct relationship between the concentration of negative energy and the amount of blocked life force flowing through the body. It often can be seen in one's posture, mannerisms, and gait. Strong chakras stand erect and powerful, and weak chakras sink inward. Notice the ways those around you protect their weak chakras in the positions they assume or the way they present themselves.

The whole energetic system can be blown out over time, directly affecting self-realization. True happiness exists when the energetic system is aligned, bright, and flowing with unimpeded life. Can you remember a time when you could fall to your knees in deep gratitude, or feeling so happy that you will burst open and joy will spill out all around you? No? That is about to change. All energies can be cleared, aligned, and renewed. Because we are made of energy, we can change energy. It is only energy. If you are thinking about all the reasons that this is crazy and could never work for you, take a moment and jot down those thoughts for future reference. These are just thoughts that your chakras are aligning to.

Each chakra occupies real estate in the body and radiates life force to every cell and thought we have. When the force of life is blocked, the chakra suffers, and pain or despair will follow. Energy is the vibration that creates the blueprint for the body. Phantom pain is proof of this. When a part of the human body is lost, such as in an amputation, sensations including pain can be perceived where the limb once was. The flesh may be gone, but the energetic design remains. The energetic blueprint can't be surgically removed.

> Kirlian photography shows the blueprint of energy beyond the physical realm. It's the blueprint of the flesh. Matter follows form.

The chakras are the blueprint of our total humanness. Each chakra corresponds to an endocrine gland, governs an aspect of our personality, and possesses a color, a sound or a tone, and a belief about how we connect to our world. We are the sum of the pieces of ourselves, and the chakras hold the unhealed inner child that is stimulated every time a similar situation or feeling occurs that originally blocked the chakra. All energies want to exist.

> When we hug another, our chakras communicate, and the hugger and the huggee connect. Notice how others hug you. Do they protect their lower chakras by withdrawing their lower body? Do they only offer you a shoulder to hug versus a whole-body hug? Do they protect their heart? Do they pat your back to tap your energy into them? Much can be learned about energy by studying the hug. Play with it and have fun.

Because energy is vibrational, including color and sound in daily life will assist healing. Chanting, toning, chimes, tuning forks, crystal bowls, and drumming are ways to include sound in your practice. Your life becomes your practice and discipline. Commit to it. Clothing, home and office décor, and colorful foods will lift the spirit and provide the color vibration that you require. We are amazing beings made of divine magnetic energy with incredible healing capacity and resilience. Take a moment to say that again. Let us take each chakra one at a time, starting at the top of the head.

The Crown or Seventh Chakra

Energy enters through the crown chakra as an open funnel. This is a direct connection to our source. The vibration here is lighter than thought because it is spiritual in nature. The crown is the union of connectedness. An open crown creates clarity and spiritual nourishment and fills the spaces within us that if were empty would result in deep craving, yearning, or despair. It holds the essence of our higher self—the part of us that knows exactly what we need and guides us to it. It is the expression of thought and the connection to higher consciousness, wisdom, and enlightenment. It is the transcendence of limitations. The crown chakra is white and violet in color and is associated with the pineal gland. This pea-sized gland regulates the hormones that are responsible for sleep. Violet is the highest vibration of all colors and is stored in the stone sapphire. Physically, it helps electrolyte balance in the body, and spiritually, it develops universal understanding. This chakra continues to develop throughout our lifetimes.

If you have never sat in silence before and breathed, here is your opportunity to give it a try. Before we begin, please know it is common to have thoughts distract you from the silence. Stillness calls forth the ego to prevent us from going inward. Thoughts flash across our minds, reminding us to pay the bills, wash the car, or get the mail. We refer to this as monkey mind. Stay with it. You are stronger than the monkey! Simply acknowledge the thought and return to the breath. It doesn't matter how many times this happens. It will lessen with each attempt.

In a quiet space, sit and relax. Close your eyes and notice the quality of your breath. Stay here a moment and simply breathe in and out in a relaxed manner. Notice how the breath goes in and out of your body. With difficulty or ease? Is it pleasant to breathe? Notice any other qualities of the breath. Once you have quieted the mind and felt your breath, bring your focus to the top of your head. Simply notice what the crown feels like. Don't try to change or control it—just feel. Stay here for a twinkling and sit in the presence of your crown. This is how we begin to discover who we are. Take note of any sensations. This is good information to build upon.

Do this with each chakra every day and witness the growth and understanding in your life. We are the opening bloom of the lotus flower.

The Third Eye Chakra or Sixth Chakra

The sixth chakra envisions us in the world between our inner landscape and the outer world. It is the seat of our intuition and creative thinking. Intense mental activity, such as crunching numbers or overthinking, can block the third eye. The color found here is beautiful shades of indigo which is the color stored in diamonds. This chakra is associated with the autonomic nervous system. It is connected to the pituitary gland and fueled by the pineal gland. The pituitary gland is the master gland in the body and controls the secretion of hormones.

The pineal gland is known as a spiritual gateway. It is located exactly in the center of the brain, and its shape resembles a pinecone. The pineal gland is quite different than other structures in the brain in that it is not paired with left and right. It is unified. Its importance is reflected in its extraordinarily rich blood supply for a tiny gland, which is the size of a grain of rice. The pineal gland contains rods and cones just as our physical eyes do. They work as light receptors, allowing this tiny gland to regulate our sleep-wake cycles by producing melatonin.

Modern diets and lifestyles calcify the pineal gland exceedingly early in life. Most lose this spiritual perception by teenagerhood. Calcification occurs through the consumption of large amounts of animal protein, fluoride, sugar, and heavy metals such as aluminum and mercury found in vaccines, pesticides, and chemicals.

Just as calcification occurs in other parts of the body, calcium is displaced from an acidic blood condition. This is a pathological condition since we are spiritually guided throughout our lives and need a healthy pineal gland. It is speculated that the pineal gland also secretes DMT (dimethyltryptamine), which has a profound effect on higher consciousness. This includes psychic vision, spiritual awakening, telepathy, and connections to divine energy. This is present when one crosses over by "going to the light" You may notice that some traditional religious leaders include the pinecone image on their staff, garb, or statues.

Interestingly, short grain brown rice is also unified as it is the only grain that is not split in left and right. It is the same size and shape as the pineal gland and historically has been eaten for spiritual benefit. Third eye atrophy is common in the modern world as spiritual practices diminish and the pineal gland deteriorates. As we open the third eye by reversing the effects of degeneration, isolation dissolves—and we become more in tune with each other and can begin to act like rice. Have you ever watched a field of grain in the wind? We see simultaneous swaying of grain like a ripple undulating as though it is one plant. Animals that have a pineal gland exhibit oneness behavior by instinctual migration and traveling in unison. This is evident when birds flock together in preparation to fly south. How did they arrange the meeting place without a cell phone? Pods of dolphins, marching locusts, ant colonies, and the march of the penguins all show the unity of mind. Have you seen the oneness of movement in a school of fish? How well are we moving in oneness with our spouses, our laws, and our leaders?

The physical eyes see the physical world, but the third eye sees the true world of a unified vision of glory.

> 🌾 Wearing sunglasses prevents the pineal gland from being stimulated by the sun and can result in insomnia or other disturbances in the sleep-wake cycle.

Throat Chakra or Fifth Chakra

Located in the center of the throat, the fifth chakra is associated with the thyroid gland. This is you at age seven to twelve. Here, we find the seat of our expression. Emotions from the lower chakras travel up to the throat to be released and expressed. Notice how when you feel sadness, it originates in your belly and moves to your throat.

As a child, I remember the feeling of a lump in my throat when being disciplined by my parents. I did not know my throat chakra was being blocked at that moment since I was not allowed to speak back, a clear example of a temporary throat chakra block. In my work in polarity therapy, I find that this chakra is the easiest chakra to be blocked.

Singing, crying, babbling, and laughing are all releases of throat chakra energy. Stay in touch with your emotions and express them as needed. We have been taught to not grunt, cry, or make inappropriate noises. Release those energies by singing in the shower, talking to yourself, or making any sound that works for you to release the throat—just get it out and clear the energy. Personally, I find singing Aerosmith songs into a makeshift microphone does it for me. Finding your voice can be difficult. As the lower chakras strengthen, your voice will diplomatically express itself to those who need to hear you because we are amazing beings made of divine magnetic energy with incredible healing capacity and resilience. The color found here is blue and is stored in the stone moonstone.

The Heart Chakra or Fourth Chakra

Ah! Love! The heart chakra is located on the central channel, slightly to the right of the physical heart, and it is linked with the thymus gland. It is a place of pure love, compassion, gratitude, and faith. Colors of pink and green are the resonance of the heart. Green is stored in emeralds and found throughout nature.

It is easy to love "good" people and "good" ideas; the practice is to open your heart and love the ugliness in the world. Is there enough love in you to do that? The heart chakra opens and closes throughout the day in response to our emotional environments. Do you spend time in a loving atmosphere or in places of negativity? The inner teenager lives here. We are a composite of ourselves at every age. If there is an unhealed part of our heart energy, it creates a hole that can never be filled in an unconscious way. Therefore, we numb ourselves with drugs, alcohol, sugar, gambling, and all the other energies that make us feel better in the moment.

The heart is associated with touch. A loving touch is a powerful act. Nurses always maintain contact with their patients through touch. I remember the day when nurses gave back rubs! Heart energy connects us to divine self-love and can also be our healing journey inward to a place of peace within the self and fill all the spaces within us with the highest vibration of love, acceptance, and truth.

When the heart is open and pulsating with life, we feel deeply connected to each other and with the beauty and harmony that surround us. We find gratitude in every aspect of our lives, including our difficulties. When the heart chakra is blocked, love is lost—and we find ourselves overwhelmed with jealousy, codependent, withdrawn, and with difficulty relating to others.

Love is the most intense emotion we experience as humans. It is limitless. Animals also have a heart chakra, meaning they are capable of love. The physical heart is snuggled between the lungs. It is through breathing that we breathe the same air as every other being on the planet. The breath I take right now may be the breath that you breathed yesterday. The heart chakra connects us all universally. Practice opening your heart makes perfect. Begin opening your heart chakra by tapping the thymus gland while repeatedly chanting:

- I have love.
- I have trust.
- I have faith.
- I have gratitude.
- I have courage.
- Love connects us all.

The thymus gland is located in the center of the chest. Do this together with your children, your spouse, or your congregation.

Solar Plexus or Third Chakra

The third chakra is where food is assimilated to create our blood. The will begins in early childhood. At around three to five years of age, we begin to put forth our ideas into the world. We will either be supported or squashed. This either blocks or opens the will chakra. It is important to find and do the work that you love to keep the will chakra in good balance.

If you have a strong sense of personal power, you have a healthy third chakra. The third chakra works closely with the third eye in an amazing way. It is part of the gut-brain axis. We have intuition and creative thought in the third eye, and the will chakra puts the thought into action. Do you know people who know what they want—and they get it? They manifest the energy through their will chakra, turning thought into action.

When this chakra is clear, we put forth our true selves into the world. When blocked, we become who we aren't. We can't turn thought into action, and our dreams remain unfulfilled. We become vulnerable to the power of others. Degeneration, such as cancer, begins by feeling powerless. We drain this chakra by not living the lives we want and living for the approval of others.

The will chakra relates to the adrenal glands. The adrenal glands are the battery power of your physical existence. Coffee and sugar exhaust these glands and blow out the will chakra. Because the liver, spleen, stomach, and pancreas are near the adrenals, digestive disorders can be addressed here. Yellow is the color of the will. Coincidentally, it is also the color of bile. Yellow is stored in the stone coral.

The Sacral Chakra or Second Chakra

The second chakra holds a lot of power because it is the deepest essence of who we are, and it stores deep emotion. The inner baby—approximately five years old—resides here. The color is orange and is stored in the stone pearl. It sits approximately an inch below the navel. Some cultures call this the *dantian* or *hara*. The ovaries are the endocrine tissue related to this chakra, but it also relates to the colon and uterus.

How we were nurtured and how we nurture others is the concept here. All issues of trust live here. All energies that ebb and flow will flow through the second chakra. Energies like love, money, generosity, life, creativity, and sexuality all flow through us in waves. Evaluate your second chakra by exploring how these energies flow through you. If one is generous with money, they most likely will be generous with affection and other energies that ebb and flow. This is the seat of our creative expression and sexuality.

Many people make decisions from this place, which houses the inner toddler. It may not be wise to let the inner two-year-old run the show and make choices that do not support life force. In my experience, all human problems involve some aspect of the second chakra.

Here is a technique to make decisions from your higher self. Sit for a few moments with your eyes closed and focus on your breath. Have a partner witness your process. Begin to sit with the problem at hand. Just sit, breathe, and relax. This may take several minutes. When you feel the rhythm of your breath and your mind is clear, imagine the solution to your problem and see it in your vision. If it is in the right direction, your partner will notice:

- the breath deepening and opening
- the heart opening and chest muscles relaxing
- the shoulders releasing
- the jaw relaxing
- the aura expanding
- facial color enhancing

The Base Chakra or First Chakra

The base chakra mirrors the crown in its funnel shape, but it points down into the earth, keeping us grounded and rooted so that nothing in life knocks us over. Our survival needs are conceptualized here, including the basic need for food, clothing, shelter, as well as the need to survive as a species. The testes and ovaries are connected to the base chakra.

Reacting to fear can block the base chakra. Many of our decisions are based on fear. We fear being alone. We fear not being accepted. We fear being unloved. We fear inadequacy, sparsity, and the unknown. It goes on and on. Make a mental list of your decisions that are made from fear. Be honest with yourself.

Surprisingly, many of our purchases are made from fear. What was the main purchase during the COVID-19 pandemic? Toilet paper! That is the base chakra's response to fear. Toilet paper relates to the organs of elimination in the second chakra. Interesting, right? It is healing to bring our unconscious thoughts into awareness. Fear is nothing more than *false evidence appearing real.*

The base chakra reflexes to the seat of kundalini—a powerful source of divine energy that sits at the end of the spine. It is a dormant source of energy and becomes "awakened" with spiritual practices such as meditation, yoga, and breathing. It is the most powerful energy in the human body. Our base chakra connects us to the physicality of life. It is through the base chakra that we connect to the planet with the vibration of the earth and each other. The color is red and is stored in the stone ruby. This chakra is fully formed by age one. When you feel safe, have healthy boundaries, and can be still, the base chakra is healthy.

In my experience, the best way to keep your chakras in good health—like all other aspects of your life—is to work at it every day, especially in times of stress. Here is a simple visualization that may take some practice at first. When you master your chakras and know what they feel like, you will be able to align and clear your energies in a snap. That may be the most powerful thing you do in your life. Changing your energy will also change those around you because we resonate with our environments. Everybody gains from your effort.

> 🌾 Air travel is dehydrating and depletes chakra energy. It is important to replenish ourselves on all levels when arriving at our destinations. A chakra alignment exercise will help.

The Daring Clearing

This is my version of a chakra alignment. I have combined several techniques for a profound experience. I share this with you in hopes of enhancing your healing journey.

Read this through first and then practice it. It is helpful to practice with a trusted partner so one can relax and perform the exercise while the partner reads the exercise aloud and then switch. You may also make a recording of your own version of this for your personal daily exercise.

Review the basic anatomy of the chakra system in order to follow the practice. Shut off your phone and create a safe place for healing. Sit comfortably with your spine in a straight position. The shushumna is the center channel that runs along the spine and flows freely when posture is aligned.

Close your eyes and focus on your breathing. Take several minutes to acquaint yourself with your breath. Explore everything in this moment: the smells, the sensations of inhalation and exhalation, the feeling of your chest, muscles tension throughout your body, and any other tangible feelings. This is only an assessment. Don't try to change anything, simply notice.

After several minutes, notice if you can feel your hair follicles or fingernails. Really focus. Notice how breath comes into your body and what it feels like to exhale. Take as much time as you need to fully relax. As though you are a spectator, watch the breath come in and out as you breathe.

When you feel a rhythm and find a relaxed state, perceive the magnificent brilliant white light above your head. Just sit for a moment and see it. It is always there. Do not go further until you really perceive this. Now sense the top of your head and gently allow the crown chakra to open. You may align your fingertips in the center of your scalp and spread the crown open with your fingers. This may feel warm or magnetic.

There is no judgment here. Only you and the energy are here. When you are ready, allow the light to come into your crown. Notice what this feels like. Take enough time to feel the sensation.

Now the brilliance of the light radiates down into your third eye chakra. Take a moment and allow the light to clear anything in its path. Fill the third eye with the light, knowing it is the power center of your creativity and intuition. Feel the softness and release between the brow. Take in a deep breath and allow any obstacle to be free. When the third eye is filled with light, return your attention to the light above your head.

The light is even more beautiful and intense. Bring your awareness deeper to visualize the light and take note of any glimmers of color. Allow the light to travel into the crown, past the third eye and into your throat chakra, and invite the light into your throat as it fills every space with its brilliance. This is the seat of your expression. Take a moment and notice without judgment or thinking what your throats needs in this moment. Let the energy do the talking as you sit and observe. Be patient, and it will come. Spend a few moments here feeling the effects of the light. Ask your throat what sound is present. It will reveal itself. Just pause here and listen. Imitate the sound. Giggling, laughter, and other vocalization release blocked energy and liberate the chakra.

Again, look above your head at the abundant source of light as it pours into your crown, through the third eye and throat. It continues down the shushumna and enters your chest and your heart chakra. Allow the light to intensify as it fills every part of your heart being. Bring to your awareness those you love and those who love you. The love is always with us. Feel its intensity. You may have physical sensations of your love. Spend a moment here bathing in the healing light of love. Allow the feelings of love to travel down your arms and into your hands. Place your hands on a place on your body that needs healing—or hold your hands out to the universe to send love to another who needs healing. Notice any sensations as energy travels within you. If any thoughts enter your mind, simply acknowledge them as thinking and return to your breathing. When you are ready, bring your focus above your head to where the light has become more vivid.

As the light travels into your crown chakra and down the shushumna, it clears anything in its path that does not serve you. It travels to the solar plexus or third chakra. Allow it to accumulate here and bring healing to your digestive organs—even if you do not know what they look like. The energy knows what to do. It fully aligns and clears your will. Reflect upon a time when your will was not supported. Feel it in your body. Allow that feeling to move through you and witness the light filling that space. Stay in is chakra until it feels complete.

The light continues into the sacral or second chakra, filling it with beautiful rays of light. Be open to receive and watch the light as it clears, cleanses, and restores balance. The deepest essence of who you are lives here. Let the light occupy your second chakra and release what no longer fulfills you. You do not have to name it—just give it freedom. Examining this area, do you see color? Take time to observe. Do you hear sound? What is the sound? Allow the sound to be set free. Invite your voice to express and free the sound. With the curiosity of a child, open all of your senses and ask if there is a message for you. Do not think of one in your mind; allow the body to present it to you. Give yourself permission to be fully present in this moment and experience your true essence. When this feels complete, return to the bright light above your head, which has become more intense.

The light radiates downward through the crown chakra, past the third eye chakra, past the heart chakra, filling the shushumna and continuing through the second chakra and into the base chakra, connecting you to Mother Earth's energy. The entire system pulsates with life energy and penetrates light into the ground, supporting you. It extends strong roots deeply into the ground and spreads out into your environment, creating a stable groundedness as mighty as a mountain. Allow time for the roots to grow. Spend several minutes here and visualize earth's energy as it enters through the base chakra and pulses up the shushumna through all the chakras and out the crown.

The simultaneous inflow of heaven's energy and earth's energy creates the pulsation of life force. Sit for a moment here and feel your life energy surging throughout your body. Allow the light to intensify as it consumes every space in your physical body. Drink it in until you are so full that it spills out around you, clearing your aura. Spend time here in a whirling bath of brilliant light. When you are ready, return to your physical body by squeezing your hands, moving your feet, and stretching. Now, open your eyes and take note of how you feel. Centered? Grounded? Whole? Clear? This is what alignment feels like. It is best to make decisions from this place.

Each day will call for less time and effort to achieve the same results until you can clear yourself in a quick moment. This practice can be embellished with toning, tuning forks, chakra bowls, or mantras. Sound and color are also vibrations and can be incorporated into your daily practice. Daily chakra clearing creates the clarity that becomes your normal state of being. It is a state of bliss—all the time! Honestly, there is not a word to describe it. The changes will be noticeable. Daily chakra alignment assists healing on all levels. It is important to understand that this exercise is not in our imagination. The light is real and is always present. It is deeply nourishing and is the sustenance to our life force.

When beginning a new practice, I find it helpful to journal any thoughts and document the changes as they occur. Once you know the feeling of being aligned, notice how long it lasts and what in your life takes you out of that state. You will find over time that your alignment sustains you through the day and becomes a natural state of being. Energy is intensified when two or more people participate. Invite others in to experience the oneness you have created, and before you know it, you will be in an energy circle!

While raising my children, I found that a chakra alignment exercise was an effective tool to control anxiety before taking tests. I recall a time when my daughter was about to perform a dance solo, and her anxiety was stealing her focus. Among the excitement of backstage happenings, I was in the wings guiding my daughter through a chakra alignment. It was a perfect performance.

A Word about Crystals

Clear quartz crystals are simply stones from the earth that magnify and clear energy. You may have one in your watch. Marcel Vogel, an IBM scientist, discovered while growing crystals, they take the form of whatever he was thinking. The intention of thought is communicated just like the crystal component of a computer chip (Marcel Vogel Legacy).

Crystals can be an integral part of healing and happiness. I choose to use clear quartz crystals because they are programmable, and I can energetically infuse them to be whatever I want them to be. You may also be attracted to rose quartz or amethyst. Whatever stone you decide to purchase, allow the crystal to choose you. Crystals have many purposes: clearing your personal space, clearing, and aligning your chakras, performing a crystal layout, or placing them around your home or office to keep the vibration high.

To begin a healing journey using crystals, it is best when done with a partner, taking turns being the receiver. To prepare for a healing session, you must be well rested and able to be fully present for your loved one. Wearing natural white cotton, the absence of color vibration will help prevent energies other than your own from sticking to you. Synthetics will create a static electricity, making it difficult to clear yourself. When working with another's energetic field, we must be in a place of alignment. The chakra alignment exercise is a good way to prepare to work with others. When we enter another's electromagnetic field, we are in the presence of divine energy and are respectful with the highest intentions. It is an honor to be in someone's energy, and we behave and think in love only.

The room should be clean and organized. Bring in high vibrations with fresh flowers, soft, healing music, and dimmed lighting. Clear the space in the room with the C side of a large crystal and set the intention to yourself or out loud. The widest side of the crystal with the shortest point is the C side of the crystal. For instance, you may say, "I call forth the highest divine light to surround this room and name of loved one. I ask for guidance, blessings, and protection that my loved one be filled with healing light now and always." Or make one up that suits you.

The receiver or loved one lies down on the floor or on a bodywork table, fully dressed, and closes their eyes. Their job is to be open to receive and simply breathe. You, the "healer," stand so that the loved one's head is at your left hand. With your left hand, connect with the energy of the loved one with a gentle contact of light touch to their shoulder.

Stay in this position for a moment until you feel your energy and your loved one's energy entraining with each other. The right hand sends energy, and the left hand receives energy. We have chakras in our palms! Slide your right hand over to the umbilicus or second chakra (belly button) and your left hand over the forehead or sixth chakra. Slowly and gently rock the body with your right hand while keeping your left hand steady.

When you feel a connection has been made, you can remove your hands. With both hands, scan the vital life force, starting at the head and ending at the toes. Hold your palms facing your loved one—one to two inches above the body—and slowly move your hands over the chakras.

Feel the magnetic pull between your hands and the body. Notice any places that feel hot or blocked. If your intuition is sharp, you may receive images or messages.

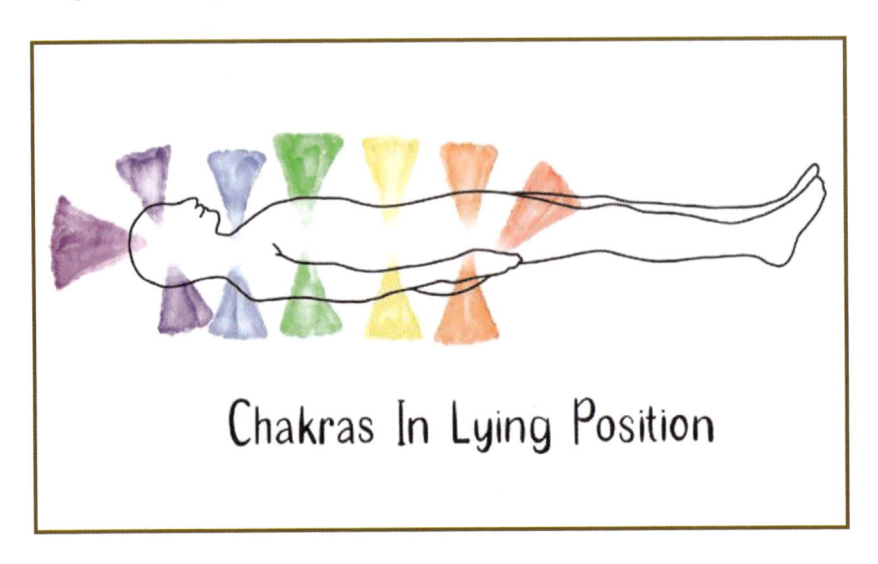

Chakras In Lying Position

To clear the field using a clear quartz crystal, hold the crystal in your right hand but never below the level of your heart. The crystal will pick up energy from your lower chakras. The C side of the crystal is used when clearing energy. Always come from a place of alignment and set the intention with love.

Hold the C side of the crystal facing outward and gently wave the crystal from left to right with the purpose of clearing low vibrations with long, intentional sweeps from the head down to the toes to clear each of the seven auric layers. The negative energy will be attracted to the crystal. Wipe the crystal after each sweep with a dry organic white cotton facecloth. Wash the facecloth when finished.

Place the crystals on the body in this order C side down: heart chakra in the center of the chest, third eye chakra between the brows, throat chakra, solar plexus chakra just above the navel, second chakra just below the navel, and base chakra at the pubic bone. Take a step back so that you are no longer directly in the healing field. Allow the energy to circulate, move, and release and clear. While you witness this, hold the intention of love and goodness.

Visualize the loved one at their highest and best and hold that energy until it feels complete. Now remove the crystals one at a time in this order: base chakra, second chakra, solar plexus chakra, throat chakra, third eye chakra, and heart chakra. Always apply the heart chakra crystal first and remove it last since it leaves the loved one in a state of love. To close the energy circuit, place your index and middle finger of the right hand on the second chakra and the index and middle finger of the left hand on the third eye. Maintain contact and bring in the energy of gratitude for the session. Now lift both hands upward, holding the position of index and middle fingers together, to the ceiling and break the contact. Allow the loved one to remain lying down and allow the energy to settle. When finished, discuss what each of you experienced and commit to confidentiality. Arrange for your turn to be the loved one for another time. It is not advisable for the loved one to clear anyone after they have been worked on.

Clear the space again to remove any negative energy that may be lingering. Wash your hands in cold water. Clear yourself with the chakra alignment exercise or with a crystal. Be certain you are not carrying your loved one's energy.

While working with anyone else's energetic field, it is important to stay out of the way to ensure their energy does not seep into you. Therefore, we align first. The longer and deeper you clear your own chakras, the deeper your clearing ability and intuitive sense will be. Begin to practice with crystals in five-minute intervals. Always end the session with a beautiful affirmation. "I love my body, and I trust its wisdom" is a one-size-fits-all affirmation that is amazingly effective. If your crystal becomes heavy with murky energy, bury it until the full moon has passed to recharge the crystal.

The earth draws out negative energy. The magnetic energy of the sun and moon charge all of us! Keep your crystals outside as much as possible or soak them in water near a window. Add a pinch of unionized natural salt to the water. Keep your crystals in natural materials like a glass plate or bowl. When the collective vibration of the crystals is at its highest, the glass container may break. I have a stash of beautiful glass plates on hand that I pick up at yard sales for that purpose.

Crystals pick up the vibrations of all seasons—so go ahead and let them play in the snow! It is best to keep your crystals in your energy only and not allow others to touch them. After using a crystal for clearing, separate it from your other crystals. Tired crystals drain clear crystals. Crystals are always clearing—even when not in use.

I have placed large clear quartz crystals in the construction of my house where I feel the energy is condensed and blocked. All houses have energetic personalities! When guests enter my home, where do you think they sit? Right under the crystal that is in the ceiling! The crystal in my kitchen seems to be where people come to complain. The crystal soaks up that energy and disperses it outside.

I use crystals in my healing every day and have found a way to keep the energy moving in my body by drinking crystalized water. Simply place an energetically clean crystal in a glass. Add pure water. Let stand overnight. You will notice the difference in taste and the energetic effects in your body.

You may want to find a qualified polarity practitioner or energy healer to experience a professional healing session and get your chakra engines tuned. The practitioner is the conduit for healing light to clear the blockages. He or she is connected to you. You are connected to your source through them. Light passes through the practitioner into you. It is the best threesome you can have.

American Polarity Therapy Association (APTA)

> 🌾 When you have mastered perceiving energy, you can place your hands over your food and feel the life force coming through or lack thereof. You will feel if your food is charged with life force or is drained.

Meridians

The center of the earth possesses a strong magnetic charge. It contains iron and other magnetic metals. It can be viewed as the earth's chakra. Through the cosmos, energy is pulled toward the surface of the earth, creating mountain ranges. The range lines can be viewed as meridians or wireless pathways that flow in defined patterns throughout the body. The seven main chakras of the body are the energy center just like the center of the earth.

Magnetic pull is created from the cosmos forming twelve pathways in the human body. Like an energy lake of the body, the chakras give rise to twelve smaller river channels of energy, called meridians, which feed and nourish every cell in our bodies. The energy bodies of chakras and meridians bring life force in the same way veins and arteries bring blood flow to cells. A meridian is a path for which life force or chi flows through. Meridians are fractal branches of energy.

Meridians work in pairs, and each meridian is located on both sides of the body:

- lung-large intestine
- heart-small intestine
- liver-gallbladder
- kidney-bladder
- stomach-spleen
- heart governor-triple heater (not shown)

The *conception vessel* or *governing vessel* is part of the eight extraordinary meridians that assist the twelve meridians to circulate vital life energy. Meridians begin and end in our fingers and toes and run throughout our bodies. Hand meridians arise at the cuticles. A manicure may look pretty, but nail polish and artificial nails block the flow of life energy.

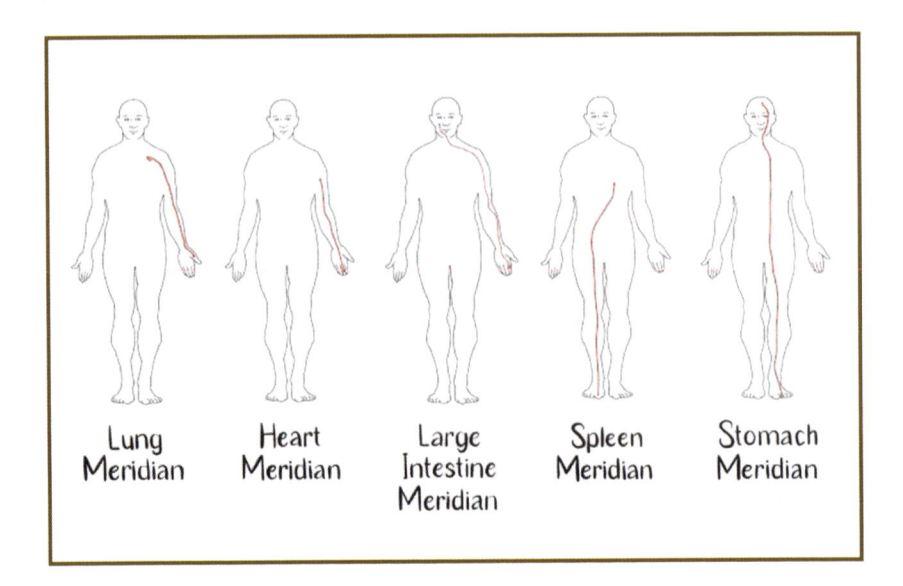

| Lung Meridian | Heart Meridian | Large Intestine Meridian | Spleen Meridian | Stomach Meridian |

| Urinary Bladder Meridian | Small Intestine Meridian | Kidney Meridian | Liver Meridian | Gall Bladder Meridian |

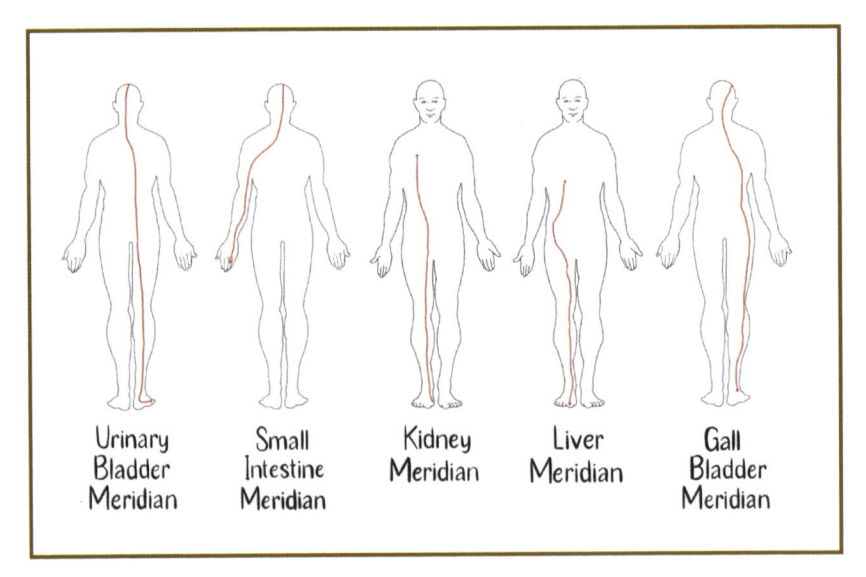

According to Traditional Chinese Medicine, every twenty-four hours, life surges through us via the meridians. Here is an example of the energy clock. Every two hours, a meridian is activated. At 3:00 a.m., the lung meridian is activated and slowly winds down at 5:00 a.m. The lungs extract clean chi or life force from the breathed air and combine it with food chi, which is then dispersed throughout the body. If you find yourself with cold hands and feet, your lung chi may be weak.

Lung energy responds well to foods with pungent flavors. When lung energy is imbalanced, we find ourselves full of grief and a defeated outlook on life. Large intestine energy emerges at 5:00 a.m. and is in motion until 7:00 a.m. Incidentally, this is the best time to have a bowel movement.

The imbalance of this meridian may be reflected in shoulder pain since this meridian runs through both shoulders. From 7:00 until 9:00 a.m., the stomach is in charge and responds to eating breakfast. This meridian forms chi from the foods we eat. The spleen and pancreas take charge from 9:00 to 11:00 a.m., which helps with digestion. The flavor of sweet vegetables is supportive to the health of the stomach, spleen, and pancreas. The spleen and the stomach send food chi to the lungs where it is combined with air chi. If this meridian falls into disrepair, we find ourselves worrying about everything!

The heart is in full swing at noon, giving us the capacity for high energy at the busiest time of the day. The heart works with the mind to regulate mental and emotional activities. Bitter flavors are adored by the energy of the heart. We instinctually know this, which is why we have so many coffee shops.

The small intestine arises after lunch from 1:00 until 3:00 to assist with digestion. The bladder energy peaks at 3:00 p.m. This is the longest meridian in the body. It runs along both sides of the spine and the back of the legs from head to heel. A backache at this hour of the day may be a result of a bladder meridian imbalance.

The kidney comes forth from 5:00 until 7:00 p.m. The kidney stores the chi you inherited from your parents. It is like a bank account. Keeping late hours or living a fast-paced party lifestyle will deplete kidney energy quickly. Spend your kidney energy wisely by living a prudent life. When it runs out, you are finished! A state of excessive fear shows that kidney energy may be weak. Creating dishes with a balanced salty taste will stabilize the kidney energy.

The heart governor comes forward currently. This meridian protects the energy of the heart like the pericardium protects the physical heart. Excessive talking, nervousness, and anxiety are results of overactive heart energy. As we settle into night, the triple heater becomes activated to separate the energetic waste. The gallbladder energy arrives at 11:00 p.m. The gallbladder and the liver work to ensure the smooth flow of all the meridians. The liver takes charge from 1:00 until 3:00 a.m. This is a time for deep repair and regeneration. Be sure the body isn't busy digesting at this time. This time is intended for restoration. Imbalances of liver energy will result in feelings of frustration, impatience, anger, and cynicism. A little taste of sour will help support healthy liver energy.

To charge your meridian battery, try some do-in exercises. Follow the lines of each meridian, and with a closed fist, tap the meridian three times with moderate force. If finding meridians on a chart is too cumbersome, just tap your entire foot, lower leg, upper leg, forearm, upper arm, trunk, head, and face. Do so on the front and back of your body. This is very energizing in the morning. You may also tap specific organs at peak energy times, according to the meridian clock.

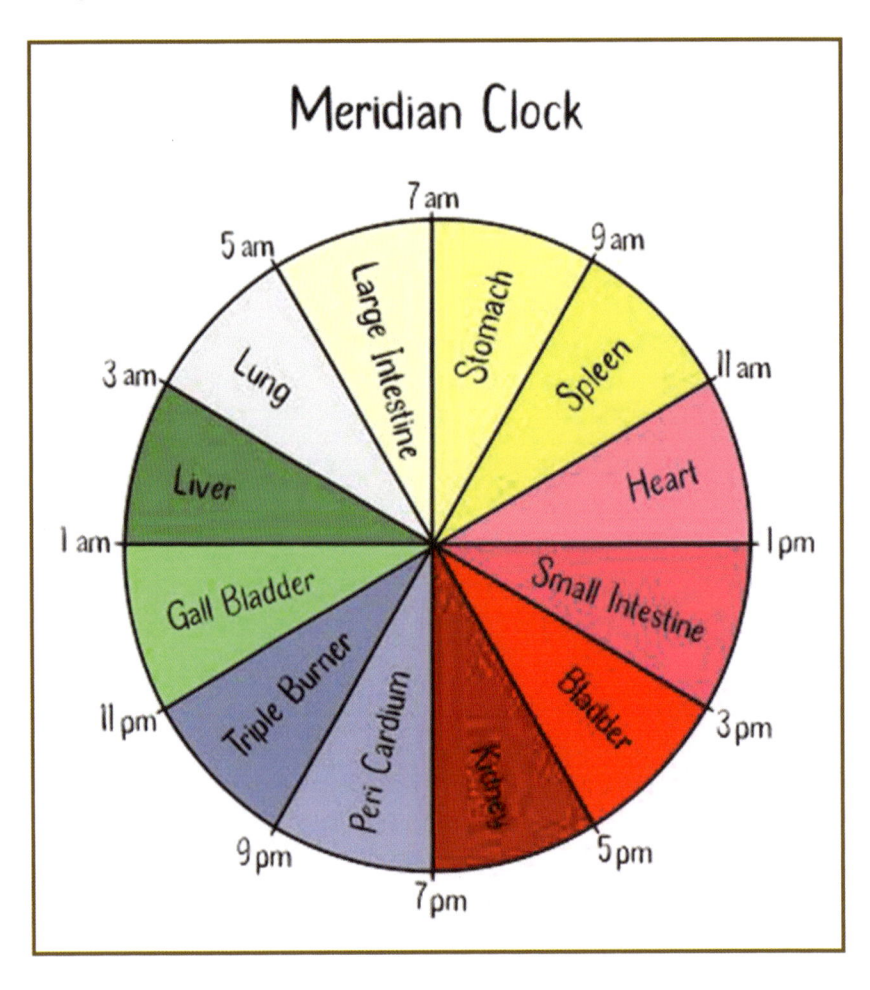

Meridian Clock

- 5 am – 7 am: Large Intestine
- 7 am – 9 am: Stomach
- 9 am – 11 am: Spleen
- 11 am – 1 pm: Heart
- 1 pm – 3 pm: Small Intestine
- 3 pm – 5 pm: Bladder
- 5 pm – 7 pm: Kidney
- 7 pm – 9 pm: Peri Cardium
- 9 pm – 11 pm: Triple Burner
- 11 pm – 1 am: Gall Bladder
- 1 am – 3 am: Liver
- 3 am – 5 am: Lung

> 🌾 Each tooth reflects to a spinal vertebra, thus the shushumna. The act of chewing alkalizes your food with saliva and stimulates your chakras. Because of this, root canals and tooth extractions can affect the whole system. Energy work or a chakra alignment after dental work will restore balance.

Chewing stimulates saliva which creates alkalization in the gut and the blood. Degeneration cannot exist in an alkaline environment. The more you chew, the more alkalizing saliva is secreted to break down carbohydrates, and the sweeter the carbohydrate becomes. Saliva is essential to healing and should be regarded as a miraculous liquid that we can make. When the body spends less energy digesting, more energy is available for healing, rejuvenation, and repair. Energy is like a bank account. Conserve it, especially as we age, and only spend what you can afford. Eating plants allows you to conserve digestive energy to realize your dreams.

The jaw muscle is the strongest muscle in the body and exerts two hundred pounds of pressure on your molars while chewing. Chew your food thoroughly until it is liquid. When you are not feeling well, chew even more—fifty chews per bite in good health and one hundred chews per bite in sickness—to activate the splendid healing fluid in our mouth.

Chapter 2

Make Grain Your Main

Eating foods that are alive from nature keeps our chakra system humming in good repair. Dead food that is packaged, canned, frozen, microwaved, irradiated, GMO, or altered in any other way leaches vital energy. Growing and eating grain holds the answers to many our personal and planetary problems.

Recent diet fads have created a nation of grain-a-phobia. Sure, processed white flour and refined grains deteriorate health, but I am talking about grain as it grows in nature with only the outer hull removed, keeping the germ, fiber, and carbohydrate intact. This is the food our ancestors ate as we evolved into the people we are today. It is human food, intended to make human cells resonate higher than animals and create thoughts with deep meaning as only humans can do.

> The Bible refers to whole grains as the "staff of life."
>
> > Behold, I have given you every herb bearing seed which is upon the face of the earth and every tree which is the fruit of a tree yielding seed. To you, it shall be food. (Genesis 1:29)

Nutritionally, whole grain is the center of good health. All varieties of grain are the best human food. Refined grains, such as white rice or white flour, oxidize quickly and lose nutrients and life force. Once the grain is cracked, the contents begins to "rust" or oxidize and will not sprout. Brown rice and whole grains have up to six outer layers of fiber to protect the inner vitamins. It takes longer to digest this fiber, thus releasing its carbohydrate slowly and maintaining a balanced state of glucose and insulin release. When glucose is balanced, our moods are stable.

Brown rice contains seventy antioxidants, including vitamin E, which can lower cholesterol. The tocotrienol (vitamin E) in brown rice has also been shown to retard tumor growth. An antioxidant neutralizes free radicals that can cause illness and aging.

Full of B vitamins, brown rice is instrumental in maintaining mental balance. B vitamins are a precursor to the production of serotonin and other happy hormones. Depression, anxiety, schizophrenia, and other emotional imbalances are influenced by these neurotransmitters. This may be why macrobiotic people are so happy.

Brown rice can also release serotonin.

Wound healing is achieved through improved blood circulation, which is created by eating grain and the breakdown of arteriosclerosis.

Brown rice contains proanthocyanins, which have been found to prevent urinary tract infections in women as well as strengthen the elasticity of arteries, which can prevent CVA (cerebral vascular accident) and heart disease and lower blood pressure.

The lecithin found in brown rice is a rich fatty acid that supports cell membranes. Remember that we are made from cells.

Brown rice is a good source of manganese, phosphorous, copper, magnesium, and niacin.

Selenium is getting much attention today for its role in reversing myelin sheath degeneration, including multiple sclerosis. Guess what? Brown rice has it.

Need not worry about breast cancer while brown rice rules your diet since it contains lignans, which studies show is a protective force of breast tissue.

Type 2 diabetes responds well to chromium, which is present in all grains. When blood sugar is regulated, so are the emotions of highs and lows.

Whole grains contain a protease inhibitor that can prevent the enzymatic breakdown of protein in the plant. Soaking and thoroughly cooking rice transforms it into a protease inhibitor that prevents cancer (Chen, 2016).

Brown rice has been used successfully in the macrobiotic treatment of cancer, migraines, anxiety, osteoporosis, asthma, depression, anxiety, dementia, and all other forms of degeneration.

All grain in its whole state is rich in fiber, making for bulky stool and stimulation of bowel function. I learned to believe that countries with small stools have large hospitals—a Kushi Institute lesson.

Rice is purchased in a dry state, usually in bulk. Dry rice never spoils, and by nature, grains do not require refrigeration, which we do not find anywhere in nature. Thousand-year-old rice will still sprout and contains its original life force. What other food gives so much life to your body? Store rice in a BPA-free container such as a mason jar. I put a bay leaf on the inside cover to prevent pests—and have not had any yet!

Much concern has been raised with the finding of arsenic in rice and for good reason. Arsenic is a known carcinogen. Lundberg Farms in California is stringent in their practices to ensure the healthiest and safest rice, which is grown on low-arsenic grounds. They publish their arsenic testing on their website. Their results show lower levels than what is considered safe to consume. Soaking rice will also wash away 80 percent of arsenic. All-natural foods—fruit, vegetables, shellfish, meat, and wine—contain trace elements of arsenic because arsenic can contaminate food from soil, water, and air.

Rice can be steamed, boiled, roasted, or pressure-cooked. Serving options are endless since rice recipes are delicious as an appetizer, main course, dessert, or snack. Rice comes in many varieties, including brown, basmati, black, red, wild, jasmine, sweet, and Wehani. Sweet brown rice has more protein and is nourishing for children. Once cooked, it can be pounded into wonderful desserts such as ohagi and mochi.

It is a good idea to soak rice in water for at least seven hours. Some cooks choose to discard the soaking water, and others do not. Personally, I do either, depending on the dish. If the flavor is in the soaking water, I keep it; otherwise, I discard the soaking water.

Rice and other grains contain phytic acid, which is considered by some as an anti-nutrient. It is how the plant stores its phosphorous to prevent sprouting. This binds with certain minerals in the body and prevents absorption. Phytic acid is deactivated by cooking, soaking, sprouting, or fermenting. When cooked, phytic acid becomes beneficial as a powerful antioxidant. Research shows that phytic acid has a strong chemoprotective activity against colon cancer—the same phytic acid that is in grain and that anti-grain diets forbid.

(Strombom, 2019)

(Society, 2016)

Grain evolved parallel to human development. When humans arrived on earth, so did grain. Most importantly, eating rice and other whole grains connects us to nature. The vibration ingested of Mother Nature is joyful, peaceful, and whole. The sacred mother is here to nourish us, and mother knows best.

Let us not wait to die to rest in peace; let us live in peace as we ingest peace. As food becomes us, we become infused with its properties. Keep that in mind with all that we eat. It seems that once we are full of the glory of grain, it is like being high on life. All the time! Each rice seed contains an awn that reaches to the cosmos, bringing in the vibration of the universe like an antenna. In fact, all grains sport an awn. This makes for the most highly charged food. This makes our thinking holistic as we feel the whole universe or see the whole picture.

If your thinking is scattered or fragmented, eating rice is for you. The rice sways in the gentle wind and bathes in the sunny field. That's the energy I want in my crazy, hectic life. A brown rice kernel contains both the seed and the fruit! Take a moment and think about that. They are one and the same. Rice has an internal plant wisdom. This is demonstrated when the farmer plants rice in water, and it sprouts upward to seek air. When planted in soil, it grows downward to root. That's impressive. The plant knows what it needs!

When we eat grain and keep our chakras aligned, we too know what we need. We hear an inner voice and the higher self directing us in life like a self-driving car. We lose that inner intuitive voice by eating slaughtered animals and junk food. Grain eating creates a universal connectedness. In fact, the concept of oneness originated in rice eating cultures. It widens our view of the world and creates global consciousness and higher human thinking. Understanding our hardships allows us to see a larger perspective of the situation. In this way, we can understand and accept our misfortunes and create the happiness we seek. We then understand why things happen to us, learn a spiritual lesson, and see the greater good. Grain thinking is human thinking with distinct clarity. Understanding our situation is a clear example of higher thinking. This is macro (grand) biotics (life). Let's act like rice.

> My teacher, Michio Kushi, was nominated for a Nobel Peace Prize for his work in spreading peace through the work of macrobiotics.

When a rice field is established, the roots entangle and enmesh each other, strengthening and supporting the whole. What if everyone took in the vibration or idea of each individual person growing into each other to strengthen the whole? Eating grain connects you to nature, which is an exhilarating feeling because nature is beautiful and real. This experience expands our thinking into universal love and connects us to each other's love. An abundance of joy and love just by eating? Yes! Get connected. Can you see how this creates stronger families? Stronger communities? Stronger countries? Stronger world? This is the premise of this book.

Anytime we grow together to strengthen the whole, we are acting like the roots of the rice plant. Let's act like rice.

Rice faces up toward heaven while it grows. It takes in the essence of the sun and the moon, forming condensed energy in the kernel. As the grain matures and becomes heavy, it bows its head downward toward the ground, taking in the strength of the earth. It is a spiritual dance of nature. Let's act like rice.

I hope you find this concept absurd enough to try eating it for yourself. The spiral nature of energy patterns is reflected in all of nature. It is called the golden ratio, divine proportion, Phi, or the Fibonacci sequence. We notice this pattern in flowers, seashells, pinecones, and fruits and vegetables, but it is present in galaxies, hurricanes and all-natural phenomena, including the human body. The human body and the entire natural world around us are a symphony of the golden ratio. This sacred ratio is 1:1.618 or rounded to 1:7. Of all the foods we eat, grain is the closest to this natural ratio. The highest species of grain, organic short grain brown rice, is the closest to the 1:7 ratio as is the human form. No other food is more perfect for humans. Maybe nature knows something. It's simple: eat nature to become nature. Let's act like rice.

> the human tooth structure has twenty molars for grinding, eight incisors for cutting vegetables, and four canine teeth for ripping flesh. Of our thirty-two teeth, four are intended to be for eating animals—4:28 or 1:7? Interesting, right?

A meal without grain is just a snack. Eliminating grain from the diet or skipping grain at a meal over time creates degeneration, inflammation, and metabolic changes. It creates isolation, and we disconnect from joy.

The Japanese character for life force is an image of steam rising from a pot of cooking rice, a valuable piece of ancient wisdom.

気

The human brain utilizes 30 percent of digested carbohydrates for cognitive function and higher thinking. A newborn can use up to 50 percent of carbohydrate calories for brain development. Grain supplies the perfect carbohydrate for brain function from infancy through our golden years.

The human tooth structure clearly demonstrates that we were intended to eat grain. Our back teeth are flat molars that are used to grind. Our lower jaw in hinged so that it creates a grinding motion on our molars. Like a mill, we grind grain into mash.

Foods that are high in fat and animal protein release an endotoxin into the bloodstream as they break down. When endotoxin levels rise, anxiety worsens. The fiber and starch in plants decreases the amounts of endotoxins absorbed into the bloodstream and reduces anxiety (Fiels, 2018).

Our alkaline saliva bathes the grain, creating perfect balance of pH. Grain is so important that amylase, an enzyme that breaks down carbohydrate is found in saliva, where digestion begins.

A nitrogen-based diet from meat fertilizes the bad bacteria in the gut and creates a condition similar to the dead zones in our waters from nitrogen runoff created from animal farming. A carbon-based diet from carbohydrates creates a clean digestive end product in the gut.

Cow's milk contains a large amount of protein intended to grow a calf into an 1,800-pound cow, and its protein proportion was never intended for humans. Cows walk immediately after birth, so its mother's milk is designed for physical development. Baby humans are carried almost for a full year because human milk is designed for brain development. Because of this, most of us can problem solve better than a cow. What other species drinks milk from another species?

In 1947, casein, the protein found in milk, was the ingredient used to make Elmer's glue; it has been replaced by less expensive synthetic ingredients. Casein makes for sticky blood, which makes for blood clotting problems, leading to stroke, deep vein thrombosis, pulmonary embolus, or heart attack. The stickiness of mucus produced by dairy allows viruses to stick to the lungs.

Compare our digestive system to a carnivore's, and you will find that our system is longer and more convoluted, allowing grain to pass within twenty-four hours. A carnivore's system is shorter because animal flesh decomposes and rots in a long, hot tube and is evacuated quickly. A carnivore's gastric pH (1–2) more acidic than ours (4–5) to digest animal fibers. Grain is much easier to digest; therefore, we do not require such a pH. Let the evidence show that humans evolved eating a predominately grain-based diet.

Cheeks! We have cheeks. Cheeks allow us to pocket food on the side while we grind. Carnivores do not have cheeks because they rip the flesh and gulp.

A dog or a lion would be delighted to feast on fresh roadkill. Would you? It is not our instinctual nature to kill. Besides, our claws and teeth are not long and sharp enough.

Let us look at animal behavior in the wild. A carnivore mates with a partner, and then they separate. They are lone hunters. A vegetarian animal lives in groups as a family with a hierarchy intelligence. The group stays together for life as it sustains and strengthens the group. They act like rice! Which behavior are we as humans emulating? Plant eaters or meat eaters?

All original cultures ate grain as their main three meals a day:

- Native Americans enjoyed corn or maize.
- Rice is native to China and Egypt.
- Wheat is known to come from New Zealand and the Middle East.
- Faro originated in Europe.
- Barley dates to biblical days.
- Asia and Africa ate Sorghum and millet.
- Oats are enjoyed worldwide.
- Rye is consumed and grown in cold climates.
- Teff is eaten in Ethiopia.

For best happiness, follow these guidelines as our ancestors did, including grain in all three meals daily.

Breakfast

Include a grain porridge and steamed greens. Leftover grain from the night before makes for a quick and easy breakfast simply by adding water to cooked grain. Since energy levels rise slowly in the morning, choose foods that are simple, soft, and easy to digest.

Lunch

Enjoy a grain dish, protein, vegetables, and greens. Protease, our protein digestive juice, peaks at noon, so lunch can be hearty and our largest meal of the day. Many restaurants and cafeterias are now serving grain bowls, making lunch outside the home convenient.

Dinner

Prepare grain, protein, longer-cooked vegetables, shorter-cooked vegetables, and greens. Make extra to create new dishes from leftovers.

Also include miso soup once or twice per day, dessert two or three times per week, and a homemade pickle once or twice per day.

Let's Act Like *Rice* | 43

A Balanced meal

It is helpful to make a double batch of any given grain and use the leftovers in other meals. A pot of grain will provide dinner, and then the same grain can be made into porridge for breakfast. Any other leftovers can be made into soup, nori rolls, stuffing, stir-fry, or croquettes. Menu planning will help with a smooth transition into a plant-based diet. A cooking partner makes this learning process a shared fun experience.

Life-Giving, Health-Building Whole Grains

Brown Rice

Brown rice comes in different varieties such as short grain, medium grain, long grain, and basmati. The energy of brown rice resonates and supports the lungs and colon. Brown rice is gluten free. Sweet brown rice is sticky, which makes it perfect for sweet desserts. Short grain is suitable for year-round enjoyment. Long grain is perfect for summer cooking. Wehani rice is a specific type of brown rice developed by Lundberg Farms in California. They are the only growers of this rice.

Millet

Millet is a tiny seedlike grain that is very nourishing for the stomach, spleen, and pancreas. It aids in healing, digestion, and glucose regulation. Usually yellow in color, millet also comes in red and other varieties. Millet is light and fluffy and takes up the flavor of whatever it is cooked with. It pairs well with sweet vegetables such as squash, carrot, or onion. For deeper flavor, millet can be dry roasted before cooking.

Millet is grown in cold weather, which creates warmth in the body, and it is especially beneficial in late summer and fall when temperatures begin to fall. A hearty grain, millet can grow under harsh conditions, which translates its energetic strength to us. It is a quick-cooking grain that requires only twenty-five or thirty minutes to cook. Millet contains lysine, an amino acid not found in many other grains and is gluten free. Millet is known for its alkalizing effect. All sickness begins with bodily acidity and inflammation. Millet to the rescue at the first sign of a cold or fatigue. Millet is very beneficial in soothing the GI system in cases of IBS, colitis, or other inflammatory conditions.

You may also find millet in your local pet supply store as some varieties are sold as birdseed.

Barley

Barley is the oldest cultivated grain. Barley nourishes the liver and gallbladder by dissolving fat. Barley has a mild cooling effect on the body and is therefore beneficial for "hot conditions" such as hot flashes, fever, or infections. When the liver is challenged by detoxifying pharmaceuticals or chemotherapy, barley can gently support liver health.

Meat and animal proteins have a contractive effect on the liver and prevent the natural upward flow of energy through the chakras and the meridians, which stagnates liver energy. You may experience this as frustration, impatience, or anger. When this is combined with the expansive nature of sugar, alcohol, or tropical fruits, the energy under pressure releases like an explosion, which is reflected in explosive behavior.

Barley has an uplifting energy that gently unblocks tension in this area of the body and creates balance in the third chakra and the liver meridian, which is reflected in kindness and a patient attitude. Hato mugi, a slightly polished barley is particularly beneficial for this. Hato mugi made into a plaster is an effective macrobiotic application for dissolving tumors. It really is an impressive grain. Barley also dissolves hardened proteins in the body such as moles and warts. The beta-glucan found in barley inhibits cholesterol production in the liver.

Incorporating barley into your diet will result in glowing skin. Hulled barley has its outer shell removed and is in its whole state, and pearled barley has had endosperm and germ layers removed, which makes it less nutritious. Barley can be slightly mucus forming so use caution with health conditions such as sinusitis, asthma, or cysts. However, on the mucus scale, animal protein, especially dairy, is the winner on mucus production. It is better to eat barley.

Quinoa

Quinoa is related to spinach and makes wonderful summertime dishes. It is considered the super grain because it is a complete protein and high in iron. Its greatly anti-inflammatory due to its high amounts of two specific flavonoids: quercetin and kaempferol. Saponin, a sticky covering, coats this grain, and it needs to be rinsed well to remove. Saponin is used in soap production and has a bitter taste. Quinoa is a complete protein, making it one of the best grains for health, and is gluten free. The stalks can be burned as fuel, and the leaves are fed to livestock. Quinoa plants also repel insects and birds.

Amaranth

Amaranth makes a warming morning porridge. When cooked, its texture is wonderfully sticky. The flavor has a hint of summer corn. The seeds can also be popped like popcorn. The harvesting of amaranth is labor intensive, and it may cost more than other grains.

Teff

Teff is a quick-cooking, gluten-free grain. Well-known in Ethiopian dishes, teff is versatile and can be prepared in many ways.

Sorghum

Sorghum grows tall like corn in the field. It has a mild earthy flavor, and its texture is similar to wheat berries. Sorghum can be used in any dish that calls for rice.

Farro

A grain from Italian heritage, farro makes wonderful dishes from simple plain grain to risottos.

Oats

Whole oats differ from oatmeal. Oatmeal is made from steaming and flattening processed oats. Oats are warming and energizing and can be strengthening in cold weather because they build ki energy. They reduce blood cholesterol levels by binding to cholesterol in the intestines, thus preventing its absorption. Oats are high in silicon, a natural element that is beneficial to bone health. Oats also create mucus—so use caution with respiratory difficulties. Gluten-free varieties are available. Using oats as an external application is soothing to the skin.

Wheat Berries

Wheat berries are the basic wheat kernel. They come in two varieties: hard red spring wheat, which is high in fiber and is used to make pastry flour, and hard red winter wheat, which is higher in protein and is used to make bread flour. It is the staple grain of the world, although usually in a processed form. Wheat can be made into plain grain for salads or flour. Crackers, bread, pastries, and packaged cereals are made of wheat flour. Once the wheat is pulverized into flour, the grain begins to lose its life force. Flour will not sprout because the spark of life deteriorated once the grain was cracked. It is best to eat wheat in its whole form. Bulgur wheat is wheat groats that have been parboiled, dried, and ground. Freekeh is wheat that has been harvested while still green and roasted to create its distinct nutty flavor.

Buckwheat

Because buckwheat grows in cold climates, it creates a deep warmth in the body. It is the most warming of the grains. Like quinoa, buckwheat is a complete protein and gluten free. Buckwheat is related to rhubarb and surprisingly not related to wheat. High in potassium, buckwheat is found as groats or flour. The groats in their whole form nourish the kidneys, bladder, bones, and reproductive pelvic organs.

Soba noodles are a buckwheat product made from buckwheat and wheat flour, which is a better option than white pasta. Kasha is buckwheat groats that have been roasted, soaked, and pre-simmered. Its flour makes for great pancake. It is a natural source of rutin acid, a flavonoid that aids in blood circulation and the regulation of blood pressure. Because of the contractive energetic force of buckwheat, it is not recommended in the treatment of some cancers.

Corn (Flint or Dent)

Native to America, corn was once known as maize. Corn husks are used to make tamales and medicinal teas. The kernels are sweet and starchy to humans (and worms). Taco shells and chips are made from corn flour.

Grits, hominy, and polenta are also corn products. Most corn produced in the United States is used to feed livestock, but it is also used in the manufacturing of paint, textiles, paper, and plastic.

Rye

Known for making beer, rye is usually eaten as flour in bread. Cooked rye has a distinct flavor that is not liked by many. Triticale is a grain that is a hybrid of wheat and rye.

Kamut

Kamut is a strain of wheat and is usually served as a hot cereal. Kamut has been shown to balance both male and female hormones and support bone health. Its buttery flavor pairs well in pilafs, casseroles, and salads.

Spelt

Spelt can be easily substituted for wheat and is easy to digest. Spelt is usually used as flour to make pasta.

Highfalutin Gluten

Today's wheat is not the same wheat our ancestors ate. Heritage wheat is tough and fibrous, and modern people are accustomed to eating squishy white bread. Because refined flour is preferred, manufacturers have given us what we want. Modern wheat has been hybridized to the point of creating new proteins, and the proteins are in exceedingly high amounts. Domesticating and crossbreeding make the wheat easier to mill and resistant to pests. It extends the shelf life, but it makes it difficult to digest. This accounts for the increase in gluten sensitivities. Interestingly, those intolerant to gluten in America can enjoy pasta and bread in Europe where wheat is more original. You can also find wheat in lipstick, sunscreen, postage stamps, toothpaste, and many personal care products.

Need another reason to make grain your main? Let us take a moment and visit where your meat source comes from. Let us first look at beef.

The high demand for fast food has created a demand for beef beyond the humane capacity of production. It has created farmed factory animals. No longer is the cow allowed in the pasture to graze. They are kept in dark buildings on dirty slab floors. They never breathe fresh air or go into the sunshine. The large amount of feces is difficult to keep up with, and it accumulates around the cow's hooves. They are tied to a post, sometimes by a nail in their nose, because their living quarters are very confined.

Since it is more profitable for a cow to reach maturity quickly, they are injected with growth hormones and steroids. The filth in which they live breeds disease, which requires heavy doses of antibiotics. Did you know that approximately 70 percent of all manufactured antibiotics are used for this purpose? If you think you don't take antibiotics, think again. We eat them every day as animal products. Is this the source of antibiotic-resistant superbugs in humans? The high-speed kill lines are so fast that many cows are hung and slaughtered while still alive. They feel the fear and scream in the slaughterhouse, which none of us will hear because of the remote locations they are housed in. The horrific conditions in which our meat is produced is protected from our awareness because laws prevent the filming of slaughterhouses. We, as consumers, would make choices based on what we see, affecting profit margins. They are called ag-gag laws (Oppel, 2013).

Factory farm workers attest to the images of cows with tears and fear in their eyes. The conditions of a factory farm make a puppy mill look like a spa (A Call For Compassion Toward Animals, 2016).

These animals fight for their lives to the very end. The cows' stress and terror trigger a surge of adrenaline into their muscles as a survival mechanism. We eat that vibration of fear, anger, and adrenaline along with the steroids, growth hormones, and antibiotics. These hormones surging through our blood relates us to the slaughter and affects our thoughts and behaviors. This is clear by turning on the news—another act of aggression, shooting, anger, or fear. Remember, as food becomes us, we become imbued with its properties. The result of the animal's acute stress manifests within us as constant fight or flight. This condition includes symptoms of anxiety, high blood pressure, palpitations, weak digestion, headaches, insomnia, and exhaustion. Sounds like many of the challenges my clients face.

Because we are holistic beings, ingesting the vibration of animals does not only affect us physically—it also disturbs our thinking. Animals blindly follow whoever leads them. Do not go through life being herded like a sheep or a cow.

To keep the cows reproducing, they are artificially inseminated by a sharp needle entered rectally to inject the bull's sperm into the reproductive system of the female cow. This procedure is painful for the cow and performed in a room known as the rape rack.

If dairy is your love, you should know the pain and sorrow the mother cow feels when her baby is taken away immediately after birth. They will never see each other again. Why? The calf is not allowed to drink her milk; that is for humans! The baby will live in a crate so small that it cannot stand or turn around. The muscles are not allowed to develop because that would make our veal tough and chewy. Mom cries actual tears and wails for months as witnessed by factory workers. When she can no longer keep up milk production, she is impregnated again and again. How many babies does she grieve before her ultimate slaughter? She was born into a system for financial gain, used and abused until the ultimate horror. They live extremely sad lives, and the energy of sadness is transmitted into her milk. Because of the high demand for cheese, the cows are always in milk production, which causes the udders to become infected. The excessive milking of the cow causes painful chronic mastitis. More than fifteen species of pathogens can be found in milk such as mycoplasma, Corynebacterium, pseudomonas, staphylococcus, streptococcus, E. coli, and brucella. The Food and Drug Administration allows 750 million pus cells to be present in each liter of milk. Think of that next time you are enjoying ice cream.

The pig's life is even more horrific if you can imagine. They live in confining cages, never see sunlight, and have open wounds from trying to move about in their confined metal cages. They live in filthy conditions on concrete floors. Many are deprived of water weeks before slaughter because they are commodities and not sentient beings. Many animal advocates show up when the pig truck arrives at the slaughterhouse to offer a drink of water before their trip to the electrocution floor. The screams are real as the pigs are beaten to conform to go to the kill floor.

We may think there is no harm in eating eggs but think again. Every time you eat an egg, a baby chick dies. Because only female chickens have monetary value, the boy chicks are tossed into a tube that leads to the shredder. This is called chick culling. The baby chicks are ground up alive. The girl chicks go to live in a dark cage in extremely crowded conditions. Several chickens are placed in each small cage. They peck each other for survival until they are debeaked to prevent fighting. Many chickens die on the bottom of the chicken pile in the cage. Some birds fall through the bottom of the cage from the weight of other birds in the pile and slowly drown in the feces below.

Again, high-speed kill lines are terrorizing to watch as the chickens are hung in an assembly line for slaughter. It is procedure that the slaughtered chicken ends up in a vat of water with other slaughtered chickens. Because of the fecal contamination from the chickens, this is referred to as fecal soup (Medicine, 2019)

Rabbits, frogs, ducks, and goats for food are treated the same way. You can find many videos and documentaries on this subject. You may find in your search that the terms "free range" and "cage free" are misleading. These terms are vague and poorly enforced. Be encouraged to learn the facts of where meat from the grocer comes from. The truth may show that animals are unjustly regarded as commodities and are treated in a way that horrifies us. Farm animals are smart, loving, and no different than the dogs we snuggle with.

Here is a point to ponder. If you were hungry, and someone handed you a pig and a knife, could you do the deed? Most of us would say no. Because the slaughterhouse and butcher package it up neatly for the grocery store, we are far removed from the killing and unaware of the animal's suffering—but that does not change a thing for the animal.

It is important to have gratitude and reverence for the animals we do eat. Demonstrate this by not wasting a drop of meat or any animal product that gave its life to us. Notice how much food is trashed at restaurants, parties, and events. Animals then suffer for nothing, and we continue to live in an unconscious way.

Since I have been advised to not show any images on this matter of animal farming, it's up to you to research for yourself. We would never allow a dog or cat to be treated like this. Farm animals are intelligent, loving, and playful, and they want to live just like you or me. They are the same as the pets we cuddle with on the couch or invite into our beds. As a child, I was fascinated by the idea of loving my dog but eating a cow.

It never made sense to me, but in elementary school, I was taught about the four basic food groups—and animal meat was on the chart. Also, my church taught me that animals are here for my pleasure and that the holy men ate meat. Besides, all my friends ate meat, and it was common behavior to eat meat. I figured that was because that was how it is supposed to be; the animal simply gives his life for us. The cow on the milk carton looked happy, so I drank it.

We have been fed a belief that only supports the profits of big business. When financial gain replaces the best interest of the people, we are dealing with animalistic thinking as is true in animal agriculture. My first awareness of animal abuse came from watching the movie *Temple Grandin*. It's a true story about an autistic woman who could relate to the cow's emotions at the slaughterhouse and positively changed how animals were raised in this country.

I became vegetarian, but I continued to eat animal by-products and fish until one evening my family and I went to dinner at a Japanese teppanyaki restaurant where they cook the food in front of you. I ordered the lobster and enjoyed the talent the chef displayed. The lobster was brought out alive and was placed on the screeching hot grill. Water was squirted on it, and a stainless-steel bowl was placed over it to steam. I watched the bowl jump and clatter until it stopped. The lobster definitely did not give its life over freely.

The lasting change came when I made grain my main and connected to the beauty of life. Life that I do not have the right or desire to abuse. Life that is precious and I live in every day. Life pulsates within us and around us. With maturity comes life experience, and my grain way of thinking has led me to never wish to harm another.

It even disturbs me to listen to my neighbor's dog bark day and night. Animal suffering is all around us. Have you seen the manicure from Russia where live ants are encased in acrylic nails? Even the ant deserves freedom from cruelty. Would you use a keychain with a live turtle in it?

Let's Act Like *Rice* | 53

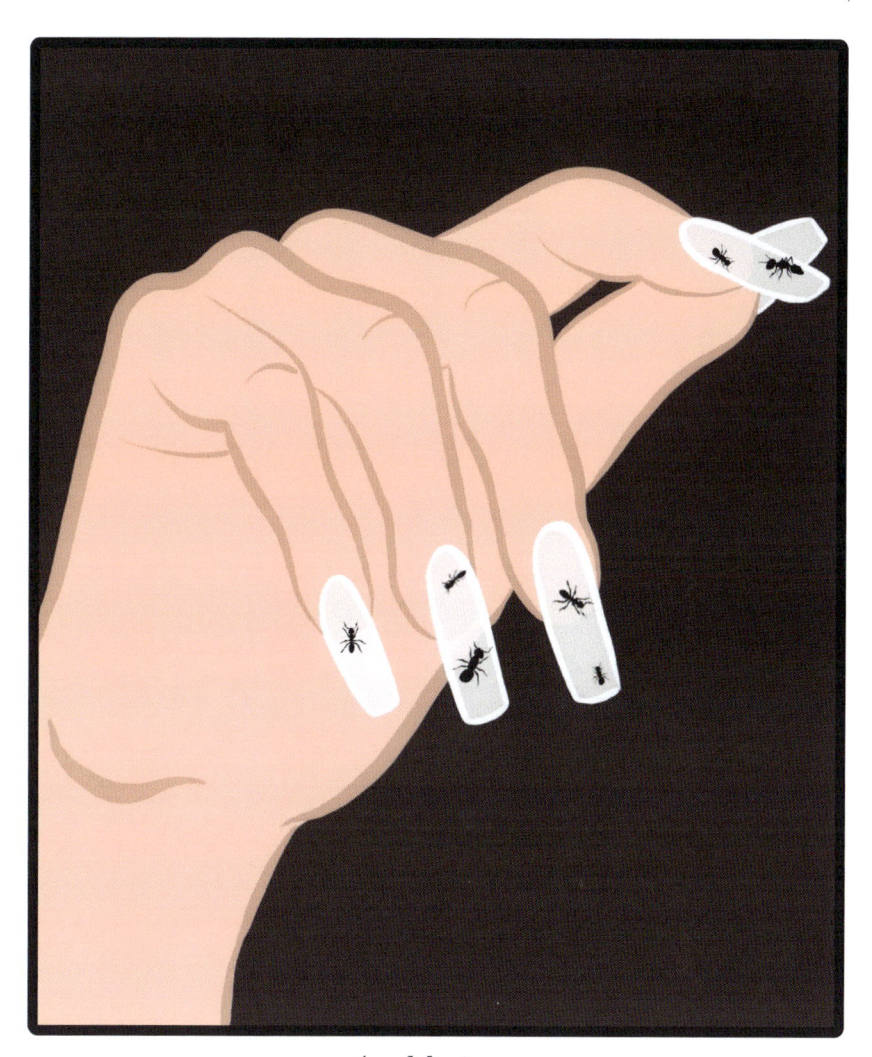

Ant Manicure

    Doesn't every living creature deserve to live freely? I believe it is our birthright. I hear people say how much they love animals. Do we really? Why do we love and rescue dogs and cats, but we slaughter cows and their babies? When we feel the oneness of the world, we feel their pain and suffering. Let's act like rice.

    Upstate New York offers several animal sanctuaries where animals are rescued and brought to a home where they can be properly cared for. Here are places that you can visit, hear their stories, and spend time with the animals:

- www.mountainhorsefarm.com
- horsesofproudspirit.org
- goatsofanarchy.com
- casanctuary.org
- www.goatlandia.org

Let us look at the effects eating animals has had on the planet. Livestock farms are responsible for more deadly greenhouse gases than all forms of transportation combined. These gases accelerate global warming, resulting in climate change. Approximately 90 percent of deforestation is caused by animal farming and palm oil production, and 110 animal and insect species are lost every day because of this.

It takes 160 pounds of grain to produce one pound of beef. Feeding a meat eater requires 3.25 acres of land each year and uses four thousand gallons of water, but a vegan uses one-sixth of an acre and three hundred gallons of water.

A few more interesting facts: 680 gallons of water are used to produce one gallon of milk and twenty-four thousand gallons of water will produce one pound of beef. Soy uses 240 gallons of water to produce one pound of tofu.

Five hundred million tons of animal manure from factory farms is introduced into the environment every year. The manure is stored in waste lagoons and sprayed into the air over fields. The toxins from the manure are breathed in by people living in the area, creating health hazards. The runoff from lagoons contaminates our rivers, lakes, and groundwater, and 40 percent of American waterways fail to meet the minimum clean water standards.

In the past fifty years, dead zones have doubled in our oceans. In them, life can no longer exist because of animal waste pollution. Our oceans are in trouble, making fish an unsustainable food. It is projected that wars over clean water are in our future. By making grain your main, you will be at the forefront of changing the planet. Actions speak louder than words or wearing ribbons. How else will we leave the earth cleaner than we found it? How will future generations enjoy nature as we know it?

As a child, my dad took us camping in Maine every summer. By the lady's bathhouse, there was a graffiti carving on the wooden door. I saw it several times a day. It read: "Let no one say and say it to your shame that all was clean here until you came." It never meant much to me until today.

Eating a plant-based diet can save your personal and planetary health. Dr. Collin T. Campbell published the largest nutritional study that demonstrated that animal protein, specifically casein, the protein found in dairy, is directly related to cancer risk. When casein consumption rises above 10 percent of calories, cancer cells are tuned on. When casein consumption falls below 10 percent of calories, cancer cells are turned off. You can find this valuable information in *The China Study* by Collin T. Campbell. It turns out that dairy does not do a body good(Campbell, 2005).

Here is a list of valuable resources for factual references of the treatment of animals and the production of animal foods.

- The Human League: Instagram
- The Humane Society of the United States: Instagram
- Mercy for Animals: Instagram
- The Save Movement: Facebook
- Plant-Based News: Facebook
- Compassion Over Killing: Facebook
- Vegan Green Planet: Facebook
- *Cowspiracy: The Sustainable Secret*: Netflix Documentary
- PETA
- *In Defense of Food*: Netflix Documentary
- *What the Health*: Netflix Documentary
- *Dairy is Scary*: YouTube
- *Forks Over Knives*: Documentary
- Food Empowerment Project
- *Vegucated*: Documentary
- *The Game Changers*: Netflix Documentary

There is no reason today to eat meat or dairy except for pleasure. We no longer live hard physical lives that require dense animal protein. Most of us are sedentary and live in the modern world of convenience. Plants offer superior protein—and every nutrient your body needs. There is a growing body of research showing the health benefits of eliminating animal protein from the diet.

Plants regenerate our bodies, alkalize our blood, and stop inflammatory processes. Inflammation is the beginning of all degeneration and the stage before cells change into cancer. Try eliminating animals from your diet for one month. Then, include animal in one meal and notice the effects it has on you. Frequently, people voice concerns that a plant-based macrobiotic diet may be deficient in protein, calcium, or vitamin B12. The macrobiotic diet has been scrutinized by disbelievers and have found that it supplies more than the requirement of nutrients. It is evident that our hospitals are not filled with nutrient-deficient vegans. If you are concerned about nutrients, include a supplement.

If it is acceptable to kill sentient beings for food, it empowers us to bring that thinking into other aspects of life. We feel free to kill everything! Killing bugs, spiders, weeds, and rodents makes it easier to kill oceans, mountains, and each other. How will we ever act like rice and come together peacefully while killing is our practice? We must change our attitudes about all animals and practice nonviolence.

Universal consciousness is changing, and we are seeing more vegan athletes, cooks, and celebrities. The Physicians Committee for Responsible Medicine is a nonprofit group of 150,000 doctors and supporters advocating a plant-based diet to restore health and prevent disease. Their motto: "Meat is the new tobacco."

In a peaceful world, greenhouses would replace slaughterhouses. I suspect that future generations will find it uncool to eat abused animals. I wait for that day. Enough said.

(Physicians Committee for Responsible Medicine, 2020)

Chapter 3

Thy Own Biome

Keeping your chakras in good repair with the high vibration of love and grain will create a strong microbiome in the gut. Millions of bacteria lie on the surface of our skin and in our mouths, nasal passages, eyes, ears, and all other mucus membrane surfaces. These bacteria create a pH to keep us protected from pathogens that cause disease.

Every species has its own special biome that supports its life. Snakes, birds, and fish have a biome. Ants and other bugs have their own bugs that keep them living. The human biome has been uniquely created for us by our ancestors' genes and the germs that surround us. A mother can identify her baby by smell and vice versa because of our human biome. Deep within our bellies, there lives a planet of life called the *gut microbiome.* Millions of bacteria and viruses and their genes create our immune systems and most of our neurotransmitters. The human biome is an individual vital organ just like our kidneys or liver. Losing that biome is just as serious as losing a kidney or liver. Each species of microbes that lives in our gut, exists for one or two days, dies off, and new ones emerge. This makes the biome easy to change. Science is now finding that a diverse bacteria pool is necessary in the prevention of illness, which we know from hundreds of years of Traditional Chinese Medicine and Ayurvedic practices. A healthy ratio of bad bacteria to good is 1:7. Have we seen this ratio before?

All health, including mental health, begins in the gut. There is a direct correlation between what goes on in your intestines and what goes on in your mind. This process is called the *gut-brain access*. It is via the longest nerve in the body, the vagus nerve, that this connection exists. When the biome is damaged, and the diversity of bacteria is low, it is reflexed to the brain. The gut has also been called the second nervous system or the *enteric nervous system* for this reason.

The gut-brain axis is a two-way street in which neurons in the intestines send signals to the brain and from the brain to the intestines. Have you ever noticed that when we have a migraine (head), we have nausea (gut) to accompany it? When we are nervous (head), our stomach (gut) is in a knot. When we are stressed (head), we lose our appetite (gut). When we spin until we are dizzy (head), we become nauseated (gut). IBS, gluten intolerance, and leaky gut (gut) are associated with depression and anxiety (head).

Have you ever noticed the connection in your body? Keeping the gut healthy keeps your emotions uplifted. Approximately 80 percent of the neurotransmitter serotonin is made in a healthy gut. Autism, depression, anxiety, dementia, and other emotional disturbances can be found lying in the key of digestion. What is really eating you is what you are eating. A strong biome is another reason why macrobiotic people are so happy. Here are a few offenders of your biome: sugar, animal protein, casein (the protein found in dairy), antibiotics, coffee, bad fats, junk food, corn syrup, antibiotics, steroids, aspirin, ibuprofen, acid-reducing drugs, chlorination, fluoride, glyphosate, antibiotics, alcohol, marijuana, growth hormone, toxic metals (found in vaccines), and triclosan (found in hand sanitizer). Yes, antibiotics are mentioned twice because they are that harmful! The list is even more extensive but let us not get overwhelmed. You may notice that none of the offenders come from the unprocessed natural world of plants. By simply paying attention to what is in the products we eat, we can protect our biome for lasting happiness.

The environmental germs that surround us in our everyday life create our biome. Visiting a new location enriches our biome, simply by breathing in the air and the bacteria native to it. Try breathing in the biome near a waterfall, the deep woods, or a meadow. Enjoying the outdoors nourishes the gut.

It is all in the label, Mabel. Are you a label reader? Although not all ingredients are disclosed on a package, a food label gives a good indication of the quality of the product. The nutrients are clearly stated on the label per serving. It is a column of the nutritional profile based on a 2,000-calorie diet. Protein, carbohydrate, vitamins, fiber, fat, and calories are clearly stated, but the ingredient list can read like a chemistry book. Here are a few things to avoid preserving our precious biome:

- Sucrose, fructose, dextrose, lactose, maltose, galactose, maltodextrin, and high-fructose corn syrup are names for sugar.
- Soybean, corn, vegetable, safflower, sunflower, cottonseed, and palm oils are inexpensive, highly processed, rancid, and highly refined oils. They are extremely inflammatory. They also raise the cholesterol in the body by creating irritation in the arteries, which triggers the release of cholesterol to respond to the inflammation. These oils are the cheapest quality available. Extremely high temperatures remove the oil from the plant except when they are expeller pressed. The neurotoxin hexane is the solvent that is used to extract the oil, and its residue has been found in these oils.
- Caramel color is a known carcinogen and weakens the gut.
- Carrageenan destroys gut bacteria, causes bloating, IBS, and is a carcinogen.
- Yeast extract is another name for MSG. They both affect the biome.
- Natural flavors contain a long list of toxic chemicals used to stimulate happy centers of the brain. For example, a natural food such as an apple is altered, modified, and chemicalized to achieve the flavor desired and is considered a natural flavor. There is nothing natural about natural flavoring. They offend the gut.
- BHA and BHT are endocrine disruptors and are not gut friendly.
- As well as gut invaders, artificial colors can produce behavior problems, ADHD, asthma, and thyroid cancer. Ditch anything artificial.
- Enriched white flour is flour made from wheat berries that have been bleached and stripped of the bran, germ, and fiber, leaving only the endosperm, which digests like sugar. The natural nutrients have been lost in the process. The flour is enriched

- to add back the nutrients. White flour takes a lot of digestive fuel to break down, especially when baked, and makes for an unhappy biome.
- Trans fats, hydrogenated oils, nitrites, nitrates, and monoglycerides and diglycerides all have harmful health effects to our biome.

Be wary of the outer food package making claims of "all natural" or "multigrain." These are all marketing ploys to entice you to buy their products. The food labels and ingredient lists will tell the true story. A product can say whole grain on the package and enriched white flour on the ingredient list, meaning there is not a drop of whole grain in the package. Read everything that you buy, eat, or serve your family.

Our modern lifestyle is killing our natural lifestyle. Studies show that a weak biome correlates with weight gain as the gut attempts to maintain homeostasis. Do we see this in real life? As a new nurse in 1982, I had never heard of bariatric medicine or seen large stretchers or wheelchairs. However, the modern diet has created a malnourished condition. The body tries to correct the imbalance and sets up cravings, hoping we will eat the foods to create a new biome. Consuming more eggs, dairy, and sugar further deteriorates the biome. It is a vicious cycle that leads to degeneration, obesity, and more suffering.

Our biome is so important that recent studies show that babies born vaginally have the benefit of traveling through the mother's vaginal biome. They have a more diverse microbiome than cesarean-born babies. Babies born naturally have the benefit of passing through the birth canal. During the birth, the baby gulps the mother's vaginal biome, setting up the baby's biome. Babies born by cesarean are more likely to have constipation (Taketoshi Yoshida, 2018).

The biome found in our mouths contains a bacterium that converts nitrates from the diet into nitrites, which are converted into nitric oxide through digestion. This compound dilates blood vessels, improves blood flow for heart health, and lowers blood pressure. Every cell in the body responds to an increase in blood volume. This brings more nutrient-rich blood to all the organs and removes debris in the process. The increased blood flow then supports erectile tissue needed for sexual arousal. If you want a healthy sex life, skip the mouthwash.

Mother's milk contains a specific indigestible sugar. This sugar creates a bacterium that lines the GI tract in infancy, which creates the child's microbiome for a healthy life. After that, it is up to us to maintain it.

What makes a strong biome? Three especially important ingredients: prebiotics, probiotics, and psychobiotics. A probiotic creates a diverse bacterium environment, and a prebiotic is the food that the gut bacteria eat. A psychobiotic is a gram-positive live bacterium such as Bifidobacterium and lactobacillus, which has a strong effect on mood, anxiety, and depression. It is the way the gut talks to the brain. All plant-based foods, particularly grain, are the perfect high-fiber, prebiotic food for your little gut creatures to thrive on. Building the biome takes a little more effort.

Miso is a highly nutritious concentrate of fermented beans and grain. Miso is by far the best food to create a healthy biome. It is best eaten every day throughout the year. An unpasteurized organic miso that has been aged for eighteen months eaten twice a day will help rebuild the gut. Miso eaten once daily will maintain your gut in good health.

Miso is a food that is so beneficial to health that it could require a prescription. Fortunately, it does not, and you can purchase good quality miso at your local health food store or online. Miso comes in a variety of flavors and bean/grain combinations. Sweet white miso is a lighter miso made with white rice. There are soy-free and grain-free misos as well. They all have great health benefits, but my recommendation for health is barley miso. Barley miso is made from soybeans and barley. It is inoculated with koji, a fermentation agent made from the aspergillus enzyme and aged in large barrels over time like a fine wine. South River Miso Company in Conway, Massachusetts, is my favorite brand.

Why do I think so highly of miso?

- Miso is a fermented soy and bean paste that has been aged for eighteen months to three years. Fermentation makes the bacteria we need in our gut. This is crucial to gut health, mental health, and overall health.
- Miso contains a large amount of natural living enzymes and lactobacilli. It contains 160 strains of beneficial bacteria! It contains glutamine to promote the regrowth of the gut lining.
- The dipilocolonic acid in miso chelates heavy metals, including strontium, from the blood.

- Miso contains a proteolytic enzyme that degrades complex allergen proteins that assist in reducing allergy triggers.
- Miso contains arginine, which increases the immune response to cancer cells.
- Miso has many antioxidants to combat free radicals.
- Miso is a good source of B vitamins, calcium, copper, phosphorous, and protein.
- Miso is anti-inflammatory.
- Miso facilitates the absorption of calcium.
- Miso is a natural antacid.
- Miso alkalizes the blood with the essential fatty acid linolenic acid.
- Miso reduces radioactivity. Hatcho miso (made from 100 percent soybeans) was imported to the Chernobyl nuclear site for this purpose.
- Miso cleanses the body of nicotine.
- The phytoestrogens in miso balance hormones related to cancer. Hundreds of clinical studies show strong evidence in the prevention of breast cancer by eating miso (Yamamoto S, 2003).
- Miso contains ethyl ester, which is an antimutagen against inflammation and cancer.
- Genistein, an isoflavone with anticancer properties to decrease tumor growth, is also found in soy. It is present twenty times more when fermented, such as in miso.
- Miso contains daidzein, a naturally occurring compound and has been shown to relieve menopause discomfort, osteoporosis, lower cholesterol, and reduce hormone-related cancers such as breast cancer (Kushi, 2001).
- Miso reduces the incidence of heart disease by lowering cholesterol and normalizing blood-clotting defenses (Yoshihiro Kokubo, 2007).
- Miso stimulates digestive enzymes and aids in digestion.

Although miso comes in many flavors, barley miso is best for daily use. Barley miso is made from whole soybeans and barley. Barley miso is a complete protein and may contain vitamin B12.

When miso is fermented over four seasons, it picks up all the heavenly and earthly energies over the year and is charged with the vibrations of nature.

A versatile food, miso is diluted and added to soup to make broth. It can also be used as a marinade or dressing.

The daily "dose" of miso is 1/2–1 teaspoon of miso per cup of liquid in a recipe.

Do not boil miso because it will disrupt the natural living enzymes and bacteria. Miso is a live food.

Be sure your miso is organic, unpasteurized, and aged ate least eighteen months.

Miso will introduce you to the wonderful flavor of umami.

All original cultures fermented specific foods for health. We instinctually knew that fermenting food made good bacteria for digestion. This is a valuable tradition that has recently been lost. Macrobiotic foods such as tempeh, shoyu, natto, kimchi, amazake, umeboshi plums, sauerkraut, pickles, and miso create a strong biome. I recommend eating a tablespoon of homemade fermented vegetable pickles daily (recipe to follow).

Fermented vegetables balance deficient and excessive hydrochloric acid in the stomach. This can be beneficial in the presence of acid reflux. The fermentation produces acetylcholine in the gut to stimulate peristalsis (the muscular contraction of the colon). This is beneficial in the presence of some forms of constipation. It also releases digestive juices and enzymes from the stomach, pancreas, and gallbladder to aid in digestion. When digestion is strong, health and happiness will follow due to the gut-brain connection. Eating fermented foods inhibits the growth of superbugs. In fact, sauerkraut was used in the 1950s to combat typhoid fever.

Be careful when purchasing fermented products. Very few store-bought products offer high-quality goods, and they usually contain sugar. It is always best to make your own fermented vegetables. It is simple to do and greatly beneficial for health.

Chapter 4

Our Reflection

What if I told you that these changes will make you look more youthful? Aha! I got your attention. Eating grains and vegetables will bring better results than any high-priced moisturizer or beauty treatment. Here is why. The energy of facial meridians distinguishes areas of the face that correlate to our organs. By simply looking in the mirror, we can assess our health and make changes accordingly. Don't like those wrinkles around the eyes? Make them disappear by eating for stronger kidney health. The science of physiognomy or facial diagnosis will reveal the truth about our health. What we see in the mirror from day to day reflects what we ate yesterday and the days prior. In fact, early detection of disease can be identified years before the occurrence simply by examining your face. The face does not lie. Our bodies reveal the truth.

The hairline shows the condition of the urinary bladder. It should be free of wrinkles, pimples, and sweat. When mucus accumulates in this area, the skin in this area will correspond.

Lines on the forehead should only appear when the brow is raised and then return to baseline regardless of age. If wrinkles accumulate here, there may be weakness in the central nervous system. Hard-baked flour from cookies and crackers can also weaken the intestines, which is also seen here.

The eyes are the overall window to health because the digestive, nervous, and urinary systems develop in utero at the same time as the eyes. When these organs become stressed by contractive animal foods, poor-quality salt, sugar, and bad fats, the condition can be seen as red horizontal lines in the sclera of the eye. Grain and vegetables will clear that up.

Black spots in the sclera are indicative of a more serious problem, showing stagnation, cysts, kidney stones, or tumors. The sclera should be white and clear. If it is cloudy or tinged with yellow, it is an early indication that mucus is forming in the gallbladder. If the sclera has a bluish-gray tinge, the kidneys are becoming sluggish from animal fat and salt. When the sclera is a cloudy brown color, it is time to rethink the diet because all the organs are affected. When the border around the iris is a milky white, it is time to check your cholesterol.

The area beneath the eye shows the story of the kidney-adrenal energy. Kidney energy is the powerhouse of reserved vitality. It is the body's internal battery. Puffiness or dark circles is symptomatic of kidney weakness which is depleting the body's vital life force. It gets depleted by travel, too much sexual activity, an imbalanced diet, lack of sleep, and stress. Reversing the cause and keeping the kidneys warm will reverse this condition. Iced drinks, ice cream, and other cold foods cool the blood, extinguish the digestive fire, and affect the kidney energy.

When fingernails are brittle, thin, or splitting, kidney energy is impaired. This is especially true in cold weather because our kidneys need warmth.

When the body is sweetened with sugars and stimulants, the eyes become sensitive to light, and we blink more.

The condition of the liver can be seen between the brows. Tightness or contraction in the liver will create one or two vertical lines here, which indicates that energy is not flowing through the liver smoothly. This can result in impatience, frustration, or anger. When liver energy is sluggish, we wake up with "sand" in our eyes. Notice its color. If the sandman brings a yellow discharge, cheese is the offender; if white, dairy is in excess. Another area to see the quality of the liver energy is the toenails.

The bridge of the nose where eyeglasses sit is the area reflected by the pancreas. If wrinkles appear here, it reveals a diet high in sugar, fat, and fruit.

The tip of the nose is the location of the heart. Is it red, puffy, or hardened? These are all early signs of trouble coming.

When wrinkles arrive above the upper lip, it illustrates an early warning of menstrual or prostate problems as well as shriveling and wasting of the reproductive organs.

The entire mouth reflects the digestive system. The upper lip reveals the stomach, pylorus, and small intestines. The lower lip shows the entire colon. If digestion is growing weak and flaccid, the lips will be swollen and pink. When the colon is contracted and stiff, they will be pale and cracked. A white band on the bottom lip shows weak circulation to the colon and correlates to anemia, which can also be seen in the nail beds. When the large intestine is inflamed, there is a slight swelling just along the lower lip line, which is where lip liner goes. The corners of the mouth are important areas to assess the valves of the colon. Recurrent cold sores are an early indication of accumulation of toxic colon material. Not to worry. Grain eating can clean it out.

The chin also reveals the health of the sex organs. Blemishes are discharges showing excess mucus and congestion from dairy. This area extends to the outer corners of the chin. Women may get a breakout here at ovulation or menstruation, showing mucus and stagnation of the ovaries.

To see the condition of the lungs, look at the skin on the cheeks. Pimples, redness, or dilated vessels show an expanded state from sugar, alcohol, coffee, spices, and other expanding foods. Dryness, chafing, and paleness show the overconsumption of dry hard-baked flour.

As animal protein is discharged from the body, hair may grow where it does not belong, costing money for its removal.

Overall dry skin or an overheated body temperature are the results of consuming all types of meat and seafood. Tuna and salmon can create enough heat to make us uncomfortably hot and irritable. Poultry drives heat deep within us, creating the same condition. If you feel tight and tense inside, this may be why. Just ask those around you.

Freckles are a way for excess sugar to be cleansed from the body. I first saw this when I took the family on a cruise. The children had free access to an endless supply of soda. Since they never had soda at home, they took full advantage. They both had freckled a few days after returning home. As cute as they were, I knew they had overindulged in sugar.

When hair turns gray before the age of fifty, be certain that minerals are being leached from the body or absent from the diet. Hair represents the outgrowth of the strength of the intestinal flora or gut microbiome.

Our conditions change every day—depending on the foods we eat. Monitor what you see in the mirror and notice your dietary changes and the correlation to the person who stares back at you. Grain and vegetable eating will soften the hardened places in the body, relax the internal organs, regenerate the places of stagnation, and hydrate and cleanse any excess. You will glow.

A good indication of the health we take in is what comes out. Let us talk about poop. Do not be squeamish—we all do it!

The human digestive system is basically a long, hot, convoluted tube that breaks down and absorbs nutrients and energy, while eliminating the waste. A healthy body eliminates at least once per day. Our diet and lifestyle greatly affect this process. Want to assess your family's health? Simply enter the bathroom after they have done their business. How is the smell? A healthy movement should have a mild aroma. That is it. If the odor leaves you running out the room for your breath, a few dietary changes are in order. Sugars, chemicals, animal flesh, and junk foods create a condition that unhealthy bacteria thrive in creating toxic waste, so to speak. We will not clench from the stench when eating grain, veggies, and other plants. In fact, all our bodily odors with become sweeter. Is it preferable to smell like a decaying carcass or a plant?

Compare your daily masterpiece to the stool chart to see where your health lies. Types 3 and 4 are healthy examples.

VIEW YOUR POO

CONDITION 1		SEPARATE HARD CLUMPS LIKE NUGGETS, DRY AND DIFFICULT TO PASS
CONDITION 2		HARD AND LUMPY, UNCOMFORTABLE TO PASS
CONDITION 3		CYLINDRICAL SHAPED WITH CRACKS AND LUMPS, SLIDES OUT EASILY
CONDITION 4		TUBE SHAPED, SOFT AND SMOOTH PASSAGE
CONDITION 5		SOFT CLUMPS WITHOUT TEXTURE
CONDITION 6		MUSHY CONSISTENCY WITHOUT DEFINED SHAPE
CONDITION 7		PURE LIQUID

Chapter 5

Get Ready

Are your chakras aligned? Are you ready to eat grain? Changing to a plant-based diet is an exciting venture with many changes awaiting you. You are about to embark on a journey of health, happiness, and inner peace. The following pages will introduce you to the basic foods to begin a balanced lifestyle. A plant-based life, including aspects of the macrobiotic diet, will change many things for you. Each person is individual. Take a moment to make a list of physical, emotional, mental, and spiritual changes that you pursue. Include the answer to this question on your list: If all things are possible, and there are no obstacles, what is my dream for my life? Don't have a dream? Give this serious thought until you find one. It may be the reason for an unsatisfied life.

Physical	Emotional	Mental	Spiritual	Dream

I am delighted to introduce you to your new world. If you have eaten the standard American diet (SAD) all your life, you may have an adjustment period to a natural diet. As your body cleanses from past eating, you will begin to discharge sugars, animal proteins, and fats. Your palate may be strongly accustomed to SAD foods. Your adaptation to natural foods is a measuring stick as to how far off the natural life you have gone. Once you have adjusted to natural foods, you will find that your taste buds come alive. The foods that you once craved will no longer have an appeal. You will appreciate the sweetness of natural foods and feel completely satisfied.

The changes from grain eating are gentle and slow. Be patient with yourself. It not like taking a pill and seeing the results in twenty minutes. You may be surprised at what you learn—and be even more surprised at the results.

These recipes will get you started on your way to blissful happiness and transition into higher consciousness of eating plants. We will unclog the body, clean out the crevasses, unwind the internal organs, breathe deeply, and enjoy the one life we have.

Most recipes make four servings. Keep in mind that a recipe is simply a guideline. These recipes can be altered to suit your own taste. Feel free to switch up the grain, vegetable, or seasonings to make it your own dish.

Always begin food prep with clean hands. Hands transmit bacteria and viruses directly into our mouths. Every time we touch our faces or take a taste during cooking, wash again. Sorry, sometimes the nurse in me comes out.

Your expression comes through the food into the bodies who eat it. Be mindful of your thoughts and attitude when prepping a meal. Shut off the TV and listen to soft music. Let the love flow through you into the food. This may be more nourishing than the physical nutrients. I understand that you may not like to cook or have much time, but cooking natural foods is the only thing standing between you and the happiness in your life. The best gift we can give to another is the art of cooking.

For best results, sort through your grain to remove any sticks, stones, or other parts of nature. Rinse the grain under running water in a colander or sieve to remove any dust. Soak the grain overnight to begin the sprouting process. Sprouting unleashes the life of the grain. In time, you may find this exciting.

In general, when cooking grain, the grain to water ratio is two parts water to one-part grain. For drier grain, use less water. For porridges, use more water. The more water, the softer the grain. Soft grain is easy to digest and ideal for breakfast, babies, and times of sickness. Place grain, water, and a pinch of salt in a heavy pot with a lid. Place kombu in a small bowl of water and soak for five to ten minutes until soft and flexible. Discard soaking water. Add soaked kombu to the bottom of the pot. Turn heat up to high and bring to a boil. Place a flame deflector or flame tamer under the pot to prevent scorching. This is good for the grain and easy to clean up. Lower the heat to low and simmer according to the recipe or cooking chart. Remove lid from pot and enjoy the happiness.

Cast-iron, enamel-coated, and stainless-steel pots get my vote. If you have never used a pressure cooker, I strongly recommend giving it a try. Pressure-cooking imparts a strength to the food that can't be duplicated by any other cooking style. The pot has a rubber gasket that seals the lid. As the liquid boils, pressure builds within the pot, heat is infused into the food, and cooking time is shortened. Beans in particular will require shorter cooking times.

Grain Cooking Chart

1 Cup Grain	Water	Simmer	Makes
amaranth	2 cups	15–20 minutes	2 1/2 cups
brown rice	2 cups	40–50 minutes	3 cups
buckwheat groats	2 cups	20–25 minutes	3 cups
farro	2 1/2 cups	20 minutes	3 cups
millet	2 1/3–3 cups	25–35 minutes	4 cups
quinoa	2 cups	15–20 minutes	3 cups

A few tidbits before we get cooking. If you wish to eliminate oil from your diet, try a sauté with broth, water, juice, vinegar, or wine. When baking, replace oil with mashed banana, avocado, soaked prunes, nuts, dates, applesauce, or canned pumpkin. Choose organic whenever possible. Not every ingredient in every recipe will say organic—but assume it is organic. Let's get going one step at a time and make the transition to eating grains a happy one.

The photos taken for this book took place in my kitchen with real food and no special effects. You will see shadows and imperfections because there are no enhancements or trickery. Real food, real dishes, and real happiness.

Chapter 6

A Grain of Happiness

Baby Dreams of Rice Cream

We, as parents, are able to launch our children into the world with the physical and emotional tools they will need to fully experience life by feeding them human food—grain of course. No need for the dehydrated, chemicalized version purchased at the grocer with the metal spout. We all know that rice cereal. It is lifeless. Nothing more to say.

- 1 cup organic sweet brown rice
- 10 cups water
- pinch of salt

....

Rinse rice in a strainer.

Place rice in a bowl and cover with water.

Soak for at least 6 hours or overnight.

Drain rice thoroughly.

Combine rice, 10 fresh cups water, and salt in a heavy pot and bring to a boil.

Place flame deflector under pot.

Lower heat and simmer for 1 1/2 hours. The power of flame energizes the grain.

Turn off heat source and let rice sit for 10–15 minutes.

Remove lid and cool rice.

Lie cheesecloth on a flat surface forming a large square 12 inches x 12 inches, overlapping if necessary. Place rice in center of cheesecloth and brings corners together.

Squeeze the rice through the cheesecloth and into a bowl.

Serve warm.

Variations

- You may substitute short grain brown rice.
- In cold weather, you may pressure-cook the rice for warmth and deeper energy.
- You may pan-toast the rice before cooking.
- Add a small amount of sweetener such as brown rice syrup or barley malt at the end of cooking for a sweeter rice. This also makes a nice pudding.
- Decrease water amount as baby grows and can eat thicker foods. Begin to include the fiber with a food mill or mouli as baby's digestion develops.
- A 1-inch piece of water-soaked kombu may be used instead of salt.
- Store rice cream in a mason jar. Reused baby food jars work fine. Lasts for one week refrigerated.
- Reheat each serving in a pan over a flame. Resist the temptation to microwave.
- Soft rice is healing for anyone when digestion is weak especially the elderly.

The greatest gift we can leave our children is the understanding of how their happiness is created.

Pressure-Cooked Rice

- 1 cup organic short grain brown rice that has been soaked in 1 1/2 cups water for 3–7 hours or overnight
- 1-inch piece of kombu soaked in enough water to cover until soft and then discard water
- pinch of salt

Place kombu on the bottom of the pressure cooker.

Add remaining ingredients, including soaking water.

Fasten the lid and bring to high pressure.

Place a flame deflector under the cooker and reduce the heat to low.

Cook for 45–50 minutes.

Allow the pressure to come down naturally.

Open lid and scoop the rice from bottom to top and serve from a wooden bowl. Enjoy!

Let's Act Like *Rice* | 75

Brown Rice with vegetables

🌾 Pressure cooking brings energy deeper into the body, creating warmth, and is best used in cooler weather.

Boiled Brown Rice

- 1 cup organic short grain rice that has been soaked in 2 cups water for 3–7 hours or overnight.
- 1-inch piece of kombu soaked in water to cover until soft (discard soaking water)
- pinch of unrefined sea salt

Place kombu on the bottom of the pot.

Add rice, soaking water, and salt.

Bring to a boil and then lower to a simmer.

Place a flame tamer under pot to prevent burning.

Simmer for 45–50 minutes with the lid on.

No peeking! The steam is revered as the spirit and can escape from the pot.

Allow the rice to meld together peacefully. Every action contains energy, which is transferred to the rice including the cook's attitude. After fifty minutes, remove the rice from the stove and remove lid. With a wooden rice paddle, scoop the rice from bottom to the top and place in a wooden bowl.

Enjoy!

> Boiled rice has a light energy and is best eaten in warm weather. What to do with leftover rice? I always make extra rice in order to make a second meal effortlessly, such as brown rice sushi rolls, stuffed squash, or Nice Fried Rice!

Nice Fried Rice

- 2 tablespoons toasted sesame oil
- 1 minced or shredded carrot
- 1 small chopped onion, shallot, scallion, or leek
- 1/2 cup chopped broccoli or any other veggie you may have in the fridge
- 2 cloves minced garlic
- 1 cup leftover cooked brown rice
- 1/2 cup frozen peas
- 1 teaspoon finely minced fresh ginger
- 1 tablespoon shoyu

In a large skillet, place oil, carrot, onion, and broccoli, and sauté until softened.

Add the rest of the ingredients and heat through.

Protein can be added to fried rice for a complete meal such as cooked or leftover tofu or tempeh. This is a good opportunity to clean out the refrigerator. Really, any chopped vegetable will do. You may substitute any grain.

> To sauté means to jump in ballet terms. Make your sauté jump by pushing the vegetables back and forth like a dance with a wooden utensil. Give it some snap and energize that rice. The love in your heart (heart chakra) travels through your chest, down your arm, through your hand (hand chakra), and into the utensil you stir the food with—so fill the pan with love.

Rice Balls

- 1 cup freshly cooked or leftover cooked short grain brown rice
- 1 package of toasted nori sheets cut into quarters
- umeboshi plums or other fillings to your liking

A rice ball is good lunchbox treat.

Form a 1/4–1/3 cup of cooked brown rice into a ball.

Press a hole in the center.

Fill the hole with a treat such as a piece of umeboshi plum, a walnut, a small piece of fruit, or even one chocolate bit.

Now dampen your hands and wrap the ball in a sheet of nori. You may need to use 2 pieces to fully cover the rice ball.

If you feel creative, you may shape the rice into triangles or other shapes.

> I learned many years later that my son traded my homemade rice balls in school with his friends all through elementary school. Many of his friends wanted the rice balls, and he held out to the highest bidder.

> Umeboshi plum is a pickled apricot type of Japanese plum. It is a powerful medicinal food in the macrobiotic healing diet. Umeboshi plum aids digestion and strengthens the blood. Its citric acid content is ten times greater than lemon juice, providing an antibacterial quality. Umeboshi is effective in combatting fatigue as well as increasing saliva production. Most noted for its alkalizing ability, umeboshi plum is used in many digestive ailments and degenerative conditions. It has a strengthening and tightening effect on the esophageal sphincter, which aids in the treatment of acid reflux, which is so prevalent today. Ume plums decrease the pathogenic bacteria in the gut such as E. coli, salmonella, and H. pylori, and has been proven to suppress the growth of the H1N1 virus. Other benefits of umeboshi plum are its antihistamine and mild laxative effects. The polyphenols contained in these plums increase the production of collagen needed for bone density. Amazingly, studies show that eating umeboshi on a regular basis can also prevent cavities and gingivitis.

Some of the umeboshi pulp is naturally squeezed to the bottom of the pickling barrel and is used in cooking for flavor. It is referred to as umeboshi paste and does not contain all the medicinal qualities. The runoff liquid is umeboshi vinegar, which is not actually a vinegar, but umeboshi juice.

Do not throw away the pit since it serves as a delightful and healing tea when steeped in water. The pit can also be roasted in a high-temperature oven until it turns to powder. Use 1/2 to 1 teaspoon of powder as tea.

The seeds inside the pit contain vitamin B17, also known as laetrile, which is an anticancer treatment.

It has a sour-salty flavor that pairs well with grain and vegetables.

Try spreading a bit of ume paste on fresh corn on the cob. Delightful!

Roomy Rice

- 1 small minced onion or shallot
- 1 tablespoon organic sesame or extra-virgin olive oil
- pinch of salt
- 3 cups chopped fresh mushrooms or dried and reconstituted mushrooms (use a variety such as shiitake, portobello, porcini, oyster, button, or any combination of mushrooms)
- 1 cup organic short grain brown rice rinsed and soaked in 2 cups water for 3–7 hours or overnight and drained.
- 2 cups mushroom or vegetable broth
- splash of organic white wine
- 1 postage stamp-sized piece of kombu soaked in water until soft (discard water)
- 6 sprigs fresh thyme
- bed of steamed greens

In a deep pot, sauté onion, oil, and salt over medium heat.

Add mushrooms and continue to sauté for 5 minutes.

Add rice and continue to sauté so that the rice toasts a bit.

Add broth, wine, kombu, and thyme.

Cover pot with a lid and bring to a boil.

Place a flame tamer under pot.

Turn down to a simmer and cook on low for 50 minutes or until rice is soft.

Serve over fresh or steamed greens.

Barley or buckwheat can be substituted for rice. Most grains are interchangeable—so mix it up!

Roomy Rice

Barley Three Ways

- 1 cup barley soaked in 2 cups water for 3–7 hours or overnight
- pinch of salt

....

Place ingredients in pot including soaking water.

Bring to a boil on high heat.

Place a flame deflector under pot.

Reduce the heat to a low simmer for 50 minutes. Add water if necessary, during cooking.

Remove from heat and serve.

You may add this to any vegetable soup or stir fry.

Variations

- Add 1 cup of a variety of small chopped vegetables or mushrooms, an additional 1/2 cup water, and a splash of sake or white wine toward the end of cooking. Continue cooking on low heat until all ingredients are soft and water has been absorbed. Dilute 1 tablespoon sweet white miso in 2 tablespoons of water and stir into the pot. The starch from the barley will thicken the dish like a risotto.
- Add 1 cup cooked barley to any vegetable soup.
- Mix 1 cup cooked barley, 1/2 cup red onion, 1/2 cup chopped cooked spinach, and top with the dressing of your choice.

Warm Barley Salad

- 1/2 cup barley soaked in 1 cup water for 3–7 hours or overnight
- 1/2 cup wild rice
- 1 cup water
- pinch of salt

Combine barley and soaking water, wild rice, 1 cup water, and pinch of salt into a heavy pot with lid.

Bring to boil and lower to simmer for 50–60 minutes.

In a separate bowl, add

- 2 stalks finely chopped celery with leaves
- 8 trimmed and chopped snow peas
- 1/2 red apple finely chopped
- 1/3 cup pistachios

Combine barley/rice mixture with vegetables, apple, and nuts in a bowl.

In a jar, shake up a combination of

- 2 tablespoons sesame or olive oil to taste
- juice of 1 lemon
- pinch of salt

Drizzle over barley salad and serve while warm.

My four-year-old granddaughter, Delilah, loves this dish because of the delicious "a-stachios!"

Warm Barley Salad with broccoli and corn

🌾 Substitute vegetable broth for water when cooking grain. Be creative—try using green tea or apple juice.

Side Note: Any grain can be pan-toasted before cooking.

Side Note: You will never be bored of eating grains if you try combining different grains together. Try 1 cup rice and 1/2 cup barley, millet/rice, quinoa/bulgur wheat, rice/wheat berries, rice/millet/oats, on and on.

Rice Is My Vice Salad

- 2 cups cooked short or long grain brown rice (really any grain will do)
- 1/2 cup each: blanched broccoli florets
- 1 blanched chopped carrot
- 1/2 small red onion
- 1/4 cup sliced celery (include the leaves—they are delicious and have great health benefits to every bodily organ)
- 1/4 cup blanched fresh or frozen corn
- 1/4 cup soft nuts (walnut, pecan, or pine)
- handful of uncured organic olives

Mix all ingredients together. Top with Donna's Famous Dressing (page 192) or dressing of your choice.

This salad is great to bring to a potluck or gathering. It suits most people's taste buds.

Breakfast Porridge

- 1/2 cup oats
- 1/2 cup buckwheat groats
- 3 cups water
- pinch of salt
- 1 minced carrot
- 1/2 minced parsnip
- 1/2 cup minced rutabaga
- 2 teaspoons 3-year barley miso diluted in 1 tablespoon water

Place oats, groats, water, and salt in a pot.

Bring to a boil with the lid on. Lace a flame deflector under the pot. Lower to a simmer.

Cook for 15 minutes until the grain softens.

Remove lid and add vegetables. Place lid back on pot and continue to cook another 15 minutes or until the vegetables are soft.

Add diluted miso.

Turn off heat and allow miso to heat through for 3 more minutes.

This dish can be changed up by changing the grain. There are endless possibilities of grain porridges. Enjoy!

Let's Act Like *Rice* | 87

Breakfast Porridge

> 🌾 A pinch of salt is the amount of salt that fits between your thumb and index finger.

Classic Brown Rice Morning Porridge

- 1 cup short grain brown rice rinsed well and soaked in 3 cups water for 3–7 hours or overnight
- pinch of salt or 1-inch piece of soaked kombu

Place rice with soaking water and salt in a pot with the lid on.

Bring to a boil over high heat and then reduce to low.

Place a flame tamer under the pot to prevent scorching.

Simmer for 50 minutes.

Allow to sit a few minutes before serving.

Add additional water for desired consistency.

This can be made with leftover cooked rice and 1 cup water. When grain sits after cooking, it extracts the starches and makes for a creamy dish. Serve in a bowl topped with small dabs of chopped umeboshi plum and toasted pumpkin seeds. This breakfast travels well in a thermos. Keep the pumpkin seeds separate to maintain their crunch.

To quicken the cooking process, begin the night before by bringing the rice, water, and kombu or salt to a boil and then turn off the heat. Allow to soak overnight and continue cooking in the morning. Add water if needed. This is a time-saver on a busy morning.

Brown Rice Porridge

Mashed Millet

You may never want mashed potatoes again.

- 1 cup millet rinsed and soaked in 4 cups of water 8 hours or overnight. (Millet normally doesn't need to soak, but this recipe offers a very creamy texture when soaked.)
- 1/2 head cauliflower, chopped
- 1/4 teaspoon of salt
- 1 tablespoon tahini
- 1/4 cup plant-based milk
- chopped flat leaf parsley

Combine millet, soaking water, cauliflower, and salt into a pot.

Cover with a lid and bring to a boil.

Place a flame tamer under pot and cook for 30–40 minutes.

Remove the lid and mash the millet mixture until it has a smooth texture like mashed potatoes.

Add tahini and milk into a separate bowl and mix.

Add tahini-milk mixture to millet and stir to combine.

Garnish with parsley.

Top with Mushroom Gravy. (page 92)

Mashed Millet with Mushroom Gravy

Mushroom Gravy

- 2 teaspoons sesame oil
- 1/2 cup diced sweet onion
- pinch of salt
- 3–4 dried shiitake mushrooms soaked in 2 cups water until soft (keep the soaking water)
- 1/2 cup chopped fresh mushrooms
- 3–4 sprigs of fresh thyme
- 1 teaspoon minced fresh ginger
- 1 tablespoon shoyu
- 2 tablespoons kudzu dissolved in tablespoons cold water (use your fingers to mix, crush, and dissolve kudzu)

Sautee onion with oil in a skillet until soft.

Add salt.

Remove stems of shiitake and discard. They are fibrous and tough.

Chop shiitake and add shiitake and soaking water to onions.

Add all the mushrooms, thyme, and ginger.

Bring to a boil, cover with a lid, and turn down heat to low.

Simmer for 10 minutes.

Season with shoyu.

Remove thyme stems and discard.

While constantly stirring, add kudzu and continue to stir until gravy becomes translucent and thickens.

Millet with Sweet Vegetables

This dish is helpful if your moods are unstable or if you have difficulty maintaining a happy expression. Maybe your joy comes and goes, and you find yourself worrying and feeling anxious. Somewhere around late afternoon, when the sun begins to settle, blood sugar drops and the uneasy feelings and cravings of hypoglycemia appear. A little pick-me-up is in order. Millet and sweet vegetables, if eaten regularly, can regulate your blood sugar and feed your biome, keeping you in sustained happiness.

- 1 cup organic millet, rinsed
- 1 small winter squash-cut into small cubes (kombucha, butternut, buttercup, Hokkaido)
- 2 carrots cut in the same size as squash
- 1 sweet onion quartered
- 3 cups water
- 1-inch piece of kombu soaked in enough water to cover (discard water when kombu is soft and pliable)

In a heavy pot, layer kombu, millet, squash, carrot, and onion and salt.

Add water and place on flame.

Bring to a boil.

Place a flame deflector under pot.

Reduce the heat to low and simmer for approximately 30 minutes or until both millet and vegetables are soft.

Remove kombu, chop, and stir it back into the pot.

Spoon into serving dishes while slightly mixing millet with vegetables.

Before cooking, millet can be dry roasted on the cooktop for a toasted flavor.

Queen of Quinoa

- 1 tablespoon sesame oil
- 1/2 kombucha or winter squash, cubed
- 1 clove minced garlic
- 1/2 cup rinsed quinoa
- 1/2 cup green lentils, rinsed
- 1 3/4 cups water
- 1-inch square piece of kombu soaked in water until soft (discard soaking water)
- 1/4 teaspoon salt
- Chopped flat leaf parsley or scallion for garnish

Place oil and squash in deep heavy pot and sauté for 5 minutes. (Water sauté if not using oil.)

Add quinoa and lentils, garlic and stir.

Add water, kombu, and salt.

Bring to a boil with lid on.

Turn down to a simmer and continue to cook for 30 minutes.

Serve in bowls with a fresh garnish.

On a cold winter day, you may place the pot with lid on in a 350-degree oven for 30 minutes instead of on the cooktop.

Let's Act Like Rice | 95

Queen of Quinoa

Winner Takes All Millet Balls

- 1 cup rinsed millet
- 2 1/2 cups water
- pinch of salt
- 3/4 cup raw chopped almonds or pine nuts
- 2 teaspoons shoyu
- 3/4 cup dried currants
- 1/2 cup minced flat leaf parsley

In a heavy pot, combine millet, water, and salt.

Bring to a boil on high heat with lid on.

Place a flame deflector under pot to prevent scorching.

Lower heat and simmer 20–25 minutes.

Take millet off the heat and stir in almonds, shoyu, currants, and parsley.

Allow to cool enough to handle.

Roll into balls.

Let's Act Like Rice | 97

Millet Ball

Fill It with Millet

- 2 winter squashes cut in half and seeded. Acorn, red kuri, buttercup, or kombucha squashes work well.
- 2 tablespoon sesame oil
- 2 pinches of salt
- 2 cups or 1 recipe of Winner Takes All Millet Balls
- 1/2 cup grated mochi

Preheat oven to 325 degrees.

Rub the oil all over all sides of the squash and sprinkle each half with salt.

Place face down on a baking sheet.

Place in oven uncovered and bake for 1 hour or until squash is fork tender.

Stuff 1/2 cup of the millet mixture into each half of baked squash. Pile it high for a fancy presentation.

Sprinkle grated mochi over each piece of stuffed squash.

Return to oven for 15 more minutes or until mochi melts over the squash.

Serve on a bed of greens for a spectacular presentation.

Rah Rah Quinoa

- 1 cup rinsed quinoa
- 2 cups water
- pinch of salt

Place all ingredients in a pot with a lid.

Bring to a boil.

Place a flame deflector under the pot.

Lower to a simmer. Simmer for 15–20 minutes.

Cooking quinoa without a lid makes for a delightful fluffy grain. Cooking with the lid on makes the grain wetter.

Make It Red Instead

Add one small beet that has been peeled and diced at the beginning of cooking into any pot of grain for a festive and colorful dish.

Popped Amaranth

- 1 cup dry amaranth

Heat a stainless-steel skillet on medium-high heat. You've reached the right temperature when a drop of water splashed into the skillet jumps and disappears.

Add 1/4 of the amaranth to the hot skillet and place a lid on.

Shake the skillet back and forth until all the amaranth has been popped. It will release its fragrance.

Place in a bowl.

Continue popping amaranth 1/4 cup at a time.

- Popped amaranth makes a nice dry cereal served with plant milk and fruit.
- Cooled popped amaranth can be used as dry cereal and stored in a glass jar with a lid.
- Popped amaranth is a nice topping for desserts.
- Popped amaranth can be added to salads.
- Popped amaranth can be seasoned and eaten with a wet finger. Kids love this!

Breakfast Amaranth

- 1 cup rinsed amaranth
- 3 cups water
- pinch of salt
- 1 cup fresh or frozen corn
- a bit of fresh herbs, finely chopped
- Toasted pumpkin seeds to embellish

Add first 3 ingredients into a pot with a lid.

Bring to boil and lower to a simmer.

Place a flame tamer under pot to prevent scorching.

Cook on low heat for 20 minutes.

Add corn and continue cooking with lid on for 5–10 more minutes. Garnish with fresh herbs and pumpkin seeds.

Breakfast Amaranth

> It is important to buy corn that has been organically grown. Corn, soy, wheat, and sugar beets are crops that have been highly genetically altered. If it is not organic, assume it is a GMO product.

The Romance of Amaranth (Salad)

- 1/2 cup rinsed amaranth
- 1 cup water
- pinch of salt
- 2 cups of cucumber sliced into rounds (be creative here and try cucumber daisies)
- 12 snow peas, trimmed and chopped (steamed or raw—your choice)
- 1/4 cup chopped celery
- 2 tablespoons shoyu
- 2 tablespoons fresh lemon juice
- 5-inch strip of wakame soaked in water until soft
- 1/4 cup toasted pine nuts (or nut of your choice)
- 1 tablespoon lemon zest
- 4 scallions finely chopped
- thinly sliced lemon slices for garnish

Prepare amaranth by placing it in a pot with 1 cup water.

Add pinch of salt.

Bring to a boil with the lid on and lower to a simmer.

Place a flame deflector under pot to prevent scorching.

Cook on low heat for 20 minutes.

Turn off heat and allow amaranth to settle in the steam for 10 minutes. This creates a gentle calming energy to the dish.

Add shoyu and lemon juice into the amaranth and mix well.

Chop wakame and place in a bowl with cucumbers, peas, celery, nuts, zest, and scallion.

When cooled, add amaranth and toss together.

Garnish with lemon slices.

The Ballad of Farro Salad

- 1 1/2 cups rinsed farro
- 3 cups water
- pinch of salt
- 2 cups chopped baby kale or any other baby green
- 1 cup chopped kalamata olives
- 1/2 small minced red onion

Ballard Dressing

- 1/4 cup brown rice vinegar
- 1/4 cup white balsamic vinegar
- 1 tablespoon sweet white miso

Place farro, water, and salt into a pot with a lid and bring to a boil. Place a flame tamer under the pot.

Turn heat to low and continue cooking for 20 minutes or until farro is tender and soft.

Place cooked farro in a bowl and add the kale, olives, and onion.

The heat of the farro will wilt the kale.

Mix the dressing ingredients in a bowl with a whisk or shake in a jar. Top the salad with the dressing and toss to combine.

The Ballard of Farro Salad

Tote Your Oats

For the creamiest oatmeal you have ever eaten, listen to Donna.

- 1 cup organic thick-rolled oats
- 3 cups water
- 1 cup almond milk (if making oats other than breakfast, omit the milk and use 2 1/2 cups water total)
- pinch of salt

The night before, place all ingredients in a heavy pot with the lid on. Bring to a boil and shut the heat off.

Let sit overnight. This extracts the starch and makes for a creamy breakfast.

In the morning, heat the oats and stir until thick and creamy. You may need to add a little more water.

I tote my oats to work in a thermos with a variety of toppings:

- dried or fresh fruit
- chopped nuts or seeds
- strips of toasted nori
- pinch of cinnamon
- nut butters
- dried coconut
- dash of sweetener such as brown rice syrup, barley malt, or maple syrup

Since containers of nonorganic maple syrup are usually sealed with formaldehyde, choose organic.

> Leftover cooked oats are a great soup thickener.

Bucky-Wheat and Greens

- 1 cup rinsed and pan roasted buckwheat groats
- 2 cups water
- pinch of salt

- 2 kale leaves
- 2 Napa cabbage leaves
- 15 trimmed snap peas
- 1/2 sliced red onion

Dressing

- 2 tablespoons tahini
- 1/4 cup fresh lemon juice

- 1/2 teaspoon shoyu
- Water to thin dressing

Place groats, water, and salt into a pot with a lid and bring to a boil. Place a flame tamer under the pot and lower to a simmer.

Cook on low for 20–25 minutes.

Separately steam the remaining ingredients. If you have time, it is best to steam vegetables individually in order to keep the character and the energy intact of each vegetable.

Chop the steamed greens, place steamed vegetables on a platter, and place cooked buckwheat in the center.

Combine dressing ingredients and drizzle dressing on top of hot buckwheat and greens and serve.

Buckwheat Bread Instead

- 3 cups whole buckwheat groats
- 1 teaspoon salt
- 1 tablespoon sesame oil
- 2 tablespoons sesame seeds

Rinse buckwheat through a strainer and place in a glass bowl.

Add enough water to cover the buckwheat with 2 inches of water and soak overnight.

Drain the buckwheat thoroughly. It will have a slippery texture, but that is completely normal. Do not rinse away the "goop." It is necessary for making the bread.

Add buckwheat to a food processor or high-speed blender. (Hand grinding does not work here.)

Add 1 cup of fresh water and blend for a full 2 minutes.

Place the batter back in the glass bowl and cover with a clean dish towel.

Leave on the countertop for twenty-four hours to ferment.

Oil a loaf pan and sprinkle the bottom with seeds. This will be the top of the loaf when cooked and flipped over.

Preheat oven to 350 degrees and place fermented batter into oiled loaf pan.

Bake for 1 hour.

Remove from oven and cool before slicing.

This bread offers your health a complete protein and fermentation. This batter also makes great buckwheat pancakes.

The addition of cinnamon, raisins, nuts, or seeds makes a sweeter bread, and adding olives, thyme, or rosemary makes a savory bread. The combinations are endless.

The Whole Bowl

Food fads come and go. For the Buddha Bowl, Macro Bowl, or Hippie Bowl, whatever is the trend, the principle is the same. Start with a bowl of grain. Make sections on top of the grain filled with:

- a protein such as tofu, tempeh, seitan, or beans
- a cooked vegetable such as carrots, celery, brussels sprouts, broccoli, cauliflower, or squash
- raw vegetables such as cucumbers, sprouts, avocado, or pickles
- a few greens such as arugula, kale, or microgreens
- a topping of toasted nuts or seeds
- a drizzle of dressing

- 1/2 cup rinsed short grain brown rice mixed with 1/2 cup quinoa and 1/4 cup lentils cooked together in 2 1/2 cups water for 50 minutes.

Top with:

- 1/4 cup steamed carrot, then finely chopped
- 1/4 cup fresh or frozen corn heated through
- 1 handful finely shredded blanched red cabbage
- 1/2 cup chopped cauliflower raw, pickled, or blanched
- lettuce greens of your choice
- 1/2 chopped fresh peach
- 1/4 cup toasted sunflower seeds
- Topped with bellini tahini or dreamy tahini dressing
- Leftovers work well for a quick bowl. The combinations are endless, and the sky is the limit on this one. Create a bowl that matches the season, the occasion, or your mood. Choose an attractive bowl to make your whole bowl unique.

The Whole Bowl

A-Hint-a Polenta

- 1 cup organic course ground polenta
- 4 cups water
- 1/4 teaspoon salt

Bring water and salt to a boil.

Begin whisking the water and slowly add polenta.

Continue whisking until all polenta is in the pot. Don't stop whisking until polenta reaches a boil.

Turn heat to low. Slow down the whisking as polenta thickens and puffs as it cooks.

Place lid on pot and simmer 15–20 minutes, whisking every 5 minutes.

Turn off heat and allow polenta to settle.

Polenta is ready to be eaten as is or spread cooked polenta to 1–2-inch thickness on a cutting board or flat platter. Polenta will thicken as it cools. When completely cooled, cut polenta into squares or triangles.

Options

- Top with a sauté of mushroom, onions, and fresh thyme.
- Pan-fry polenta squares and serve alone or with hummus, guacamole, or beans.
- Basic cooked millet can be substituted for polenta.

Patty Cake

- 1 cup rinsed quinoa
- 1/2 cup polenta
- 4 cups water
- pinch of salt
- 1/2 cup fresh or frozen corn
- Sesame oil for frying

Soak quinoa and polenta overnight for a creamy dish or skip that step if pressed for time.

Add both grains, soaking water, and salt into a pot and bring to a boil.

Place a flame deflector under the pot and reduce to a simmer.

Cook for 20 minutes.

Add the corn and cook another 5 minutes.

Allow to cool enough to handle

Form into patties and pan-fry in a good-quality sesame oil.

Top with Supreme Sour Cream. (page 203)

Mochi puffs

- 1 mochi brick (flavor of your choice)
- Store-bought mochi comes in flavors of cinnamon, garlic, plain, green tea, or sesame.

Preheat oven to 450 degrees.

Cut squares or shapes from the mochi brick.

Bake 8–10 minutes or until mochi puffs up.

May be eaten plain or dipped into a sweetener such as brown rice syrup, flavored brown rice syrup, barley malt, fruit preserves, or lemon-walnut dunk.

> Mochi is made by pounding cooked sweet rice until it becomes glutinous, but it contains no gluten. When grated into food, it thickens sauces. It has an effect of melted cheese when broiled. It can be pan-fried or grated into a waffle iron.

Paradise Rice

- 1 cup rinsed Wehani Rice soaked for 3–7 hours or overnight
- pinch of salt
- 1-inch piece of kombu soaked in water and drained
- 1 chopped onion
- 1 tablespoon toasted sesame oil
- 2 scallions cut into 1-inch pieces (go ahead and include the root, it will nourish the root chakra.)
- green garnish

Place soaked kombu on bottom of pot.

Add rice, soaking water, and salt.

Place lid on pot and bring to boil.

Lower heat to simmer and cook for 50 minutes.

Meanwhile, sauté onion with oil and a pinch of salt in a nonstick skillet. Use the smallest amount of oil to get the job done to prevent an oily dish. Just as onions become caramelized, add scallion, and mix through. Add onion mixture to cooked rice.

Garnish with parsley, cilantro, or basil

Paradise Rice

Don't Dread My Cornbread

- 1 1/4 cup polenta or cornmeal
- 1 cup whole wheat pastry flour (you may substitute another flour if gluten sensitive)
- 1 teaspoon nonaluminum baking powder
- 1 teaspoon baking soda
- 1/2 teaspoon salt
- 1 cup almond or other plant milk mixed with 1 tablespoon brown rice vinegar
- 1 flax egg
- 1/2 cup extra-virgin olive oil
- 1/2 cup brown rice syrup
- 2 tablespoons maple syrup
- 15 ounces fresh or frozen corn

Preheat oven to 400 degrees.

Sift first 5 dry ingredients into a large bowl.

Prepare a flax egg by mixing 1 tablespoon flax seed or flax meal with 3 tablespoons hot water and stir. Allow it to sit for a few minutes to congeal.

In a separate bowl, mix oil with syrups.

Add oil syrup mixture to vinegar milk mixture.

Pour the wet ingredients into the dry ingredients.

Add the flax egg.

Stir to combine enough to remove any lumps.

Add corn to the smooth mixture.

Pour cornbread batter into an oiled loaf pan.

Bake 30–45 minutes or until an inserted toothpick comes out clean.

Chapter 7

Troupe Soup

Soups are warming and prepare the body for digestion. Soup is beneficial to gut health. Energetically, soup reminds us of our primary state or the beginning of life in utero surrounded by salty water. Sitting and enjoying soup at the start of the meal relaxes and prepares the stomach to receive food. Please have a seat when you eat.

Silly Lily's Chili

Take the chill out of your day with this vegetarian chili.

- 1/2 cup rinsed quinoa
- 1/4 cup rinsed bulgur wheat
- 1 1/2 cups water
- pinch of salt

Place all ingredients in a pot with a lid and bring to a boil.
Lower the heat to low and place a flame tamer under the pot.
Cook on low heat for 15–20 minutes.
Set aside.

- 2 tablespoons extra-virgin olive oil
- 1 small minced sweet onion to equal 1 cup
- 3 cloves minced garlic
- 1 finely minced carrot
- 1 chopped green bell pepper
- 1 chopped yellow bell pepper

Add above ingredients into a Dutch oven and sauté until tender. To this sauté, add:

- 1 1/2 cups cooked or canned organic black beans, drained and rinsed
- 1 1/2 cups cooked or canned red kidney beans, drained and rinsed
- 1 (14-ounce) can organic diced tomato
- 15 ounces organic tomato sauce
- 1 small chopped zucchini
- 2 teaspoons chili powder
- 2 teaspoons cumin
- 1 teaspoon salt
- 1 teaspoon dried basil
- 1 teaspoon dried oregano
- 1 teaspoon dried parsley

Cook on medium heat for 5 minutes.

Add cooked grain and heat through.

Additional toppings:

- supreme sour cream
- scallion
- corn
- sliced avocado
- sliced uncured black olives

Serve with Don't Dread My Cornbread. (page 115)

It is preferable to avoid tropical foods such as tomatoes and peppers and stimulating spices when living in a temperate climate. I include this recipe because there are times that eating a little nightshade is better than eating animals while transitioning to a plant-based diet. Save this recipe for special events like Super Bowl parties.

Silly Lily's Chili

> 🌾 Tomato is a member of the nightshade family and is not recommended for health building. Nightshade vegetables include tomato, potato, eggplant, peppers, paprika, cayenne pepper, tobacco, and all mushrooms except shiitake. They create an acidic condition in the blood and begin the process of inflammation.

Nightshades acidify our blood more than any other plant food. Acidic blood leaches important minerals such as calcium from our bones in order to neutralize the PH. Displaced calcium results in conditions such as kidney stones and osteoporosis. Over time, a steady diet of nightshades creates a weak blood quality and sets the stage for anything inflammatory from acne to cancer.

Nightshades contain solanine, a poisonous alkaloid that is not destroyed by cooking. Solanine affects the blood, GI tract, immune function, and the joints. Nightshade vegetables grow at night. We grow during the day and regenerate at night. Energetically, a nightshade vegetable imbalances our entire energy system. Notice they all originated in the tropics, which is an extremely hot climate. They create a very imbalanced condition in the body when consuming them in a four-season climate. If you want to enjoy nightshade vegetables, you will have to go to South America.

Gentle Lentil Soup

- 1 tablespoon extra-virgin olive oil or less
- 1/2 cup chopped sweet onion
- 1 cup organic green lentils
- 32 ounces vegetable broth
- 1–2 cups water
- 1/2 teaspoon salt
- 2 medium carrots chopped
- 1 small rutabaga, chopped
- 1/4 cup burdock root
- 1 tablespoon fresh minced ginger
- 2 tablespoons miso
- fresh herb garnish of flat leaf parsley, scallion, or basil

Add oil to a soup pot over medium-high heat and add onion.

Sauté a few minutes until onions are soft.

Add lentils, broth, water, and salt.

Place lid on pot and bring to a boil.

Lower to a simmer and cook on low heat approximately 20 minutes or until the lentils are 50 percent cooked.

Add vegetables and ginger and continue cooking 10 more minutes or until the vegetables are soft.

Remove enough broth from the pot to dilute the miso and add the diluted miso to the soup.

Turn heat off and allow miso to be heat activated for 3 minutes. Do not boil miso.

Serve in individual bowls with a fresh herb garnish.

This makes for a great potluck dinner item or buffet line dish. You may make this dish with less liquid for a thick lentil dish.

Let's Act Like Rice | 121

The Gentle Lentil

Soba Up

- 1 package organic soba noodles
- 1/2 head of green cabbage, chopped into bite-sized pieces
- 2 carrots cut into rounds, cubes, julienne—whatever you fancy
- 1/2 medium onion cut into half moons
- 1 cup broccoli florets
- 10 trimmed snow peas
- 4 cups water, kombu broth, or vegetable broth
- 1/2 teaspoon of salt
- 1 cup finely chopped greens (kale, collards, watercress, or combination of any greens that you like)
- 3 tablespoons of shoyu
- 3 tablespoons mirin

Cook the noodles according the package instructions and set aside. Pour water or broth into a soup pot.

Add salt and all the vegetables except for the greens.

Add shoyu and mirin.

Bing to a slow boil and cook until vegetables are fork tender.

Add the greens.

Turn off heat and allow greens to wilt into the hot broth.

Ladle the soup over individual bowls of soba noodles.

For a warming effect, add a squeeze of fresh ginger juice at the end of cooking.

This is an opportunity to clean out the refrigerator and use any other vegetables you have.

Soba Soup

🌾 Cutting the vegetables to the same size allows for even cooking time.

Side Note: 100 percent buckwheat noodles are gluten free. Many types of soba noodles are mixed with wheat flour and contain gluten. Be sure to read the label.

Side Note: Cooked soba noodles need to be rinsed and can be stored without absorbing more liquid. Soba is a minimally processed food and can be nourishing to the urinary system and bones. Soba noodles can be added to any vegetable sauté, salad, or stir fry.

Soba Noodle Salad

Kombu Broth

- 4-inch strip of kombu, rinsed
- 4 dried shiitake mushrooms
- 4 cups water

Add ingredients into a jar with lid.

Gently shake it up.

Let sit in refrigerator up to 2 weeks. The longer the soak, the stronger the broth.

Remove kombu and discard or finely chop it and add it to whatever dish you are making.

Remove mushrooms and reserve for another use.

Voilà! Broth!

Always have broth on hand for cooking rice, soup, or noodles. To jazz it up a bit, add 1/4 cup mirin and a tablespoon minced ginger.

To expedite the broth making, place ingredients in a saucepan and heat to simmer. Simmer 15 minutes or until broth is rich and colorful.

Shiitake mushrooms are used in the macrobiotic diet for their ability to recharge the liver. The liver is involved with hundreds of functions that are taken for granted. If you have a liver malfunction, you will develop a great appreciation for the liver. The shiitake has a diverse range of healing abilities that improves immune function to fight flu, colds, and infections. It lowers cholesterol, decreases arterial plaque, regulates glucose metabolism, cleanses the blood, and improves skin conditions. It also had has antiaging and anticancer properties. Because of its affinity for the liver, shiitake assists in the recovery of hepatitis, liver cancer, and blood-clotting disorders. Shiitakes grow during the day, but other mushrooms are considered nightshades. Show your liver some love by buying good-quality shiitakes at a reputable vendor—and your liver will love you back.

Kombu Broth

Whiskey Tofu Soup

- 4 cups kombu broth
- 2–3 pinches of salt
- 1 teaspoon turmeric for coloring
- 1 package silken organic tofu
- 1 heaping tablespoon kudzu diluted with 2 tablespoons cold water
- minced scallion or fresh herb for garnish

Place broth, salt, and turmeric into a saucepan.

Bring to a boil and lower to simmer.

Add tofu and whisk. Thus, the name. Did you really think there was whiskey in the soup? Add a shot, I won't tell anybody!

Whisking the tofu into the broth creates a curd-like consistency.

Begin to whisk the soup while adding kudzu.

Stir a few minutes or until translucent.

Serve in individual bowls and garnish.

Me So Healthy Miso Soup

- 3 cups water or kombu broth
- 4-inch piece of wakame soaked in 1/2 cup water until soft, then diced (discard soaking water)
- 1/4 cup extra-firm tofu cut into small cubes
- 2 teaspoons barley miso according to taste
- 1/2 cup minced kale
- pinch of minced scallion or parsley for garnish

Add water/broth, wakame, and tofu into a pot and bring to a boil. Lower heat to simmer and cook on low for 15 minutes.

Remove a ladleful of hot broth, dissolve the miso into it, and then add it back into the soup.

Simmer for another 3 minutes.

Do not boil miso. It will destroy the live enzymes and bacteria.

Stir in kale. It becomes become bright green quickly.

Turn off heat and serve in bowls.

Top with a fresh herb garnish.

This soup feeds the gut, feeds the mind, stabilizes the temperament, and makes you so happy and miso happy!

> Miso is enjoyed year-round by creating varieties of soups simply by changing the vegetables and the types of miso. The combinations are endless.

Miso Soup

Corny Chowder

- 5 cups water
- 1/2 cup organic polenta
- 1 cup diced onion
- 1/4 cup chopped celery
- 2 cups organic corn removed from the cob. Approximately 4 ears. Frozen can be used if fresh isn't available, but fresh is always best.
- 1/2 teaspoon salt
- pinch of minced cilantro or parsley for garnish

Bring water to a boil in a soup pot.

Slowly whisk the polenta into the boiling water, stirring constantly to prevent lumping.

Add onion and celery.

Add the cobs, if using fresh corn, and remove them at the end of cooking. They impart a lovely starch.

Reduce heat to low and simmer 3 minutes.

Add corn and salt and continue cooking 15–20 minutes or until polenta is cooked.

Serve in individual bowls and garnish.

Miso can be added at the end of cooking as an option.

This chowder can be made richer or creamier by replacing a portion of the water with almond or any plant milk.

Let's Act Like Rice | 131

Corny Chowder

Sweet Autumn Harvest Soup

- 1 sweet onion chopped
- 1/2 kombucha squash peeled, seeded, and cubed
- 1/2 butternut squash peeled, seeded, and cubed
- 2 carrots, chopped
- 1 parsnip, chopped
- 16 ounces vegetable broth
- 1/2 cup apple juice
- 1 teaspoon salt
- Seasoning of your choice: 2 teaspoons cumin powder or 2 teaspoons dried herbs
- Scallion, cilantro, or minced apple garnish

Add all ingredients except garnish into a soup pot and bring to a boil.

Turn down to a simmer and cook for 20 minutes or until all vegetables are tender.

This soup can be eaten in three ways:

- as a chunky style soup
- mashed with a potato masher in the pot and served as a thick soup
- pureed as a creamy holiday soup

Garnish with scallions, cilantro, or minced apple.

Let's Act Like Rice | 133

Sweet Autumn Harvest Soup

All Over Leftover Soup

- 3 cups water or vegetable broth
- 1 cup leftover cooked grain of any type
- 1 cup chopped vegetables of any combination: broccoli, cauliflower, onion, carrot, turnip, parsnip, lotus root, or celery (leftovers would be fine)
- 1/2 cup chopped fresh greens (kale, collards, mustard, dandelion, or watercress)
- 2 teaspoons any variety of miso

Combine water/broth, grain, and vegetable in a soup pot.

Bring to a boil and lower to a simmer.

Cook until the vegetables are soft.

Remove enough broth from the pot to dilute the miso and add the miso and the greens to the pot.

Simmer for 3 more minutes.

Serve with a fresh garnish.

No need to ever throw out leftovers. Wasting real food is a lost opportunity for health. Simply make them into something else.

Add leftover vegetables to enough water or broth to cover and heat through. Add diluted miso (1/2–1 teaspoon miso per cup of liquid) at the end of cooking. Place in a blender to puree or mash by hand and, like magic, new soup awaits you.

Garnish with a fresh herb.

Leftover Soup

🌾 Always add a fresh herb or garnish to a cooked dish to balance the energy and uplift the dish.

A Bowl of Escarole

- 1 tablespoon extra-virgin olive oil
- 2 minced garlic cloves
- 5 fresh sprigs of thyme
- 1 (4-inch) branch of rosemary
- 1/4 cup organic white wine
- 1 large head of escarole washed and chopped
- 4 cups vegetable broth
- 1 cup cooked cannellini beans, rinse if canned
- 1 teaspoon salt
- 2 teaspoons sweet white miso
- Minced parsley or cilantro as garnish

Heat the oil, garlic, and herbs in a soup pot over medium heat until garlic is fragrant.

Add a splash of wine and cook a few minutes to evaporate the alcohol.

Add the escarole and sauté for 2 minutes or until it becomes wilted.

Add the broth, beans, and salt.

Cover and simmer until heated through.

Remove a ladle of broth and dilute the miso into it.

Add miso to the pot.

Turn heat to low and let the miso do its magic for 3 minutes.

Remove stems from herbs.

Serve in individual bowls and garnish.

Let's Act Like Rice | 137

Bowl of Escarole

Déjà Vu Honeydew

This is a refreshing soup that travels well in a thermos. Enjoy on a hot day.

- 1-pound pickling, English, or baby cucumbers
- 1/2 sweet honeydew melon, seeded
- 1/2 cup flat leaf parsley
- 3 tablespoons brown rice vinegar
- 1 tablespoon fresh lime juice
- 2 tablespoons brown rice syrup
- pinch of salt

Puree or grind all ingredients together until smooth. Refrigerate and serve with fresh garnish of minced cucumber, watercress, or parsley.

> Every time we eat, we have an opportunity to create health and happiness.

Chapter 8

Team Beans

Many beans contain twice as much protein as meat does. The fiber in beans is a prebiotic food, which is necessary for happiness, and it also lowers cholesterol and blood pressure. What is most fascinating is that beans help regulate internal body temperature, which is important for many health conditions. This is especially true when trying to conceive.

Incorporating beans even into an animal-based diet will lower the risk of heart disease, cancer, and diabetes, prevent fatty liver, control appetite, and improve gut health. They are a delicious addition to a summer salad or winter stew. Add them to a grain dish for variety in your diet. Variety? Approximately forty thousand types of beans are eaten around the world.

Leftover beans can be mashed and formed into patties to be pan-fried or grilled. Cooked beans can be kept frozen for six months. Beans are purchased in a dry state. Store your beans in glass containers. Soak beans for eight hours or overnight before cooking. Lentils and mung beans are legumes that cook quickly and do not require soaking. Did you know that January 6 is National Bean Day?

Shifting to a plant-based diet with the incorporation of beans may be challenging to your digestion if beans are new to you. To avoid becoming "musical," I have tips to reduce the incidence of gas:

- Soak beans for eight hours or overnight and discard soaking water.
- Skim and discard the foam off the beans during cooking.
- Place a one-inch piece of soaked kombu to the bottom of your pot when cooking beans. Kombu helps to break down the indigestible carbohydrate that creates gas in the intestine.
- Chew thoroughly. There is only one opportunity to grind your food, and that is in your mouth. Chewing creates alkalization in the gut and the blood. Degeneration cannot exist in an alkaline environment. The more you chew, the more alkaline saliva is secreted to break down carbohydrates. When the body spends less energy digesting, more energy is available for healing, rejuvenation, and repair.

> In *The Kind Diet,* Alicia Silverstone reveals the calculation that the average healthy person expels rectal gas fourteen times per day (Silverstone, 2011).
>
> Soaking beans and grain is best if done in a glass bowl, avoiding the use of plastic as much as possible. Stick to natural surfaces for least exposure to toxins.

Beans are beneficial to health, and they support a healthy agricultural cycle. Instead of depleting the soil, beans enrich the soil with nitrogen in preparation for the next crop. They are easy to grow and make a lovely addition to any flower garden.

Red Lentils

- 1 tablespoon sesame oil
- 1 small minced sweet onion
- 1 minced carrot
- 1 small sweet potato minced (sweet potato is not a nightshade—enjoy!)
- 1 minced parsnip
- 1 small red bliss potato, finely chopped
- 1 cup rinsed red lentils
- 2 cups vegetable broth
- 1/2 teaspoon salt
- Fresh herb for garnish

Sauté onion in oil in a soup pot for 5 minutes or until translucent.

Add vegetables, lentils, broth, and salt.

Put lid on pot and cook on low heat for 30 minutes or until the lentils turn yellow and creamy and the vegetables soften. Serve garnished with fresh herbs or cooked corn kernels.

Red Lentils

Lauren's Lentil Love

Love is created in this dish as the sweet vegetables hug the grain and lentils. This is a great dish to bring to a party or potluck event.

- 1 cup brown lentils
- 1/2 cup barley
- 4 cups water or vegetable broth
- 4-inch piece of soaked kombu
- 1 bay leaf
- 1 tablespoon barley miso
- 4 medium-size carrots, sliced
- 1 cup chopped kombucha or butternut squash
- 2 sweet onions
- pinch of salt
- 3–4 minced scallions

Preheat oven to 350 degrees.

Turn on inspiring music and get into the groove.

Place lentils, barley, water or broth, kombu, and bay leaf in a pot with a lid.

Bring to a boil.

Lower heat to simmer and cook for 50 minutes.

Remove kombu from pot, chop, and return to pot.

Discard bay leaf.

Dilute miso in a bit of water and then mix miso into lentil-barley mixture.

Place mixture in a pie plate or bottom of a baking dish.

Set aside.

Place carrots, squash, onion, and salt in a pot.

Add just enough water to cook or steam.

Simmer vegetables until soft.

Puree vegetables and set aside. Add water if needed.

Add the pureed vegetables on top of the lentil mixture and sprinkle with scallions.

Bake at 350 degrees for 30 minutes.

Lentil Love

Skinny Jeans Lima Beans

The low-calorie count of eating beans will keep you looking fabulous in your favorite jeans.

- 1 cup organic baby lima beans, dry
- 1-inch piece of kombu soaked in 1/2 cup water until soft (discard soaking water)
- 1/4 teaspoon salt
- 1 1/2 cups fresh or frozen sweet corn
- 1 heaping tablespoon white miso diluted in 3 tablespoons apple juice
- 1 tablespoon minced scallion for garnish

Soak beans in enough water to cover by 2 inches overnight to soften the beans and begin the sprouting process.

Discard soaking water.

Place soaked kombu and then beans in a pressure cooker and add enough water to barely cover the beans.

Turn heat on high with lid off.

When boiling begins, foam will rise to the surface of the beans. Skim off the foam with a spoon and discard.

Place lid on pressure cooker and bring to full pressure.

Turn down heat to maintain pressure.

Place flame deflector under pressure cooker and cook for 25 minutes.

Boiling beans will require at least one hour of cooking up to this point.

Bring down pressure, lift lid, and add salt.

Bring back up to pressure and cook for 10 more minutes.

Allow pressure to be released naturally.

Add corn and cook without cover for a few minutes to incorporate.

Add diluted miso and turn off heat. Allow the flavors to meld together and activate the miso for 3 minutes.

Garnish and serve

Skinny Jeans Lima Beans

Can't Beat This Meat

- 1 small chopped sweet onion
- 2 tablespoons extra-virgin olive oil or sesame oil
- 4 cloves minced garlic
- 2 teaspoons shoyu
- 8 ounces tempeh cubed and simmered for 10 minutes in 1 1/2 cups apple juice. Remove tempeh and discard what is left of juice.
- 12 ounces cannellini beans (homemade or canned), rinsed and drained

Sauté onions with oil in a skillet until translucent.

Add garlic and sauté another minute.

Add shoyu and stir to combine.

Set aside.

In a grinding bowl or food processor, mix the tempeh and beans.

Add onions to the tempeh and beans and continue to mix until it holds together.

Use this vegetable meat for meatloaf, burgers, or shape into anything you like. The texture is soft.

It is a good stuffing for zucchini, winter squash, or mushroom caps. You can also embellish with toasted nuts or seeds.

I shaped the meatless mixture into a turkey and surrounded it with vegetables for a holiday feast. We laughed for days!

Let's Act Like *Rice* | 147

Can't Beat This Meat

Chicky Peas

- 1 cup chickpeas a.k.a. garbanzo beans soaked in 2 cups water for 8 hours or overnight (discard soaking water)
- 1-inch piece of soaked kombu in 1/2 cup water until soft (discard water)
- 2 carrots, roll cut
- 1/2 cup chopped rutabaga
- 1/2 cup cubed winter squash
- 1 small sweet onion, chopped
- 1 parsnip roll cut
- 1/2 teaspoon salt
- fresh herb for garnish

Place kombu in bottom of pressure cooker.

Add beans and enough fresh water to just cover beans.

Place over high heat and bring to a boil.

Skim off foam and discard.

Apply lid and bring up to pressure and lower heat to maintain full pressure.

Place a flame tamer under pot.

Cook for 25 minutes.

Bring down pressure and add vegetables and salt.

Bring back up to pressure and cook 5–10 more minutes.

Serve garnished as a main course.

Total cooking time for boiling chickpeas is 2–3 hours.

If the mood strikes you, crush a little of the mixture and stir it in for a creamy texture. I sometimes add dried herbs to the beans at the beginning of cooking such as thyme, rosemary, or oregano. It is easy to add miso at the end of cooking as well. Leftovers can be made into a soup by adding broth.

A Chick's Sandwich

- 1 cup cooked chickpeas or 1 (15-ounce) can of chickpeas, rinsed and drained
- 1 cubed ripe Hass avocado
- 1/4 cup chopped fresh cilantro
- 2 tablespoons chopped scallion
- 1/4 teaspoon salt
- juice of 1–2 limes or enough to moisten the mash
- sandwich bread of your choice (try an un-yeasted sourdough bread or multigrain)
- sandwich toppings, such as lettuce, sprouts, or pickle

Place chickpeas in a bowl and mash with a fork or potato masher.

Add avocado, cilantro, scallion, salt, and lime juice and incorporate into chickpeas.

Spread the mash onto sliced bread and top with your favorite sandwich toppings.

Clean Bean Salad

Eating clean is a trend that means something different to everyone. You can't get cleaner than beans and vegetables.

- 1 cup organic kidney beans, cooked
- 1 cup organic garbanzo beans, cooked
- 1 cup organic cranberry bean, cooked
- 2 cups steamed or blanched string beans, cut into bite-sized pieces
- 1/4 teaspoon salt
- 1/2 small sweet onion, grated
- 2 teaspoons umeboshi paste
- juice of one lemon
- handful of fresh flat leaf parsley, minced

If using canned beans, rinse and drain.

Combine all ingredients in a bowl and toss to combine.

The addition of corn is cooling for summer weather. The addition of ginger or ginger juice is warming for cold weather.

Clean Bean Salad

Azuki Beans and Sweet Rice

- 1/4 cup adzuki beans soaked in 2 cups water 8 hours or overnight (discard soaking water)
- 1 cup sweet brown rice soaked in 3 1/2 cups water 8 hours or overnight
- 1-inch piece of kombu separately soaked in 1/2 cup of water until soft, then discard water
- Chopped scallion to garnish

In a pressure cooker, combine the drained beans, rice with its soaking water, and kombu.

Bring up to pressure.

Place a flame tamer under the pot and lower the heat to maintain full pressure.

Cook for 50 minutes.

Turn off heat.

Allow pressure to release naturally.

Remove kombu, chop, and return it to pan.

Stir to combine.

Garnish

Scrambled Tofu

- 1 tablespoon extra-virgin olive oil or sesame oil
- 1 cup diced sweet onion
- 1 clove garlic
- 2 cups sliced baby portabella mushrooms
- 1/2 cup broccoli, finely chopped
- 1/4 cup peas, fresh or frozen
- 1/2 cup summer squash or zucchini, chopped
- 1/2 carrot, shaved with a vegetable peeler and then finely minced
- 1/4 teaspoon each of salt and dried herb of your choice
- 1 block firm or extra-firm organic tofu

In a large skillet, sauté vegetables with oil, salt, and herb until vegetables are beginning to soften.

Add garlic and stir to combine.

Crumble and squeeze tofu through your fingers into the skillet. This part is fun. Have the kids try.

Continue cooking for another 10–15 minutes.

When the tofu is cooked through, turn off heat and serve.

Serving Ideas

- Serve on a bed of polenta or millet formed into a pie plate or cupcake tin.
- Serve on a baked crust as a quiche.
- Add a pinch of turmeric to look like scrambled eggs.
- Serve over cooked soft brown rice.
- Serve on nonyeasted sourdough bread as a sandwich.
- Serve alongside tempeh bacon.

Let's Act Like Rice | 153

Tofu Scramble

Before becoming food happy, I enjoyed a bit of feta cheese on a salad or spanakopita. This recipe is as satisfying.

Tofu Feta is Betta

- 1 block extra-firm tofu
- 1 organic lemon, zested and juiced
- 1 tablespoon umeboshi vinegar
- 2 teaspoons dried oregano
- 1 teaspoon minced garlic

Press the liquid out of the tofu by wrapping it in a clean kitchen towel and placing something heavy on top. Press for 15–20 minutes for tofu to become denser by draining the water.

Place pressed tofu on cutting board and cut into shapes of desired cheese bites.

Marinate tofu bites in remaining ingredients overnight. Pressed tofu will reabsorb the marinade and the accompanying flavors.

Enjoy as you wish.

Tofu feta is a nice addition to any salad.

Tofu Feta is Betta

More Cheese Please

- 1 block extra-firm tofu
- 1/2 jar or 8 ounces miso, any flavor

Press water out of tofu by wrapping it in a clean kitchen towel and laying something heavy on top. Press for 15–20 minutes.

Cut tofu into 8 slices.

Coat all sides of the tofu with miso.

Refrigerate 3–4 days.

Remove miso and serve. Miso can be used in another dish.

More Cheese Please

Tempeh and Cabbage

- 1 (8-ounce) package of soy or grain tempeh
- 1/4 cup toasted sesame oil
- 1 medium-sized head red cabbage, chopped into bite-sized pieces
- 2 tablespoons organic Dijon mustard
- 1/4 cup shoyu
- 1 cup apple juice

....

Cut tempeh into 2-inch pieces.

Pan-fry tempeh in oil in a large skillet on medium-high heat.

Remove tempeh and set aside.

Add cabbage to skillet. Add additional oil if needed.

Sauté the cabbage until it begins to soften.

Add the apple juice on top of the cabbage and cover with lid to steam the cabbage.

When cabbage is nearly cooked through, return tempeh to pan and cook both tempeh and cabbage together.

After 20–30 minutes, cabbage should be delightfully tender.

Stir together shoyu and mustard and stir into cabbage.

Cook another few minutes to incorporate the salt from the shoyu.

Serve alongside a simple grain and salad and feel the happiness.

Tempeh and Cabbage

🌾 Tempeh is a nutrient-dense fermented soy product that offers a complete protein and a variety of vitamins, fiber, calcium, iron, and other minerals. It offers both a prebiotic and probiotic health benefit. The soybeans are fermented and broken down by microorganisms and then pressed into a cake form. Tempeh originated in Indonesia and is now enjoyed worldwide. Tempeh needs to be cooked. The nutritional makeup of tempeh shows it has an antioxidative, anti-inflammatory, and antithrombotic effects. The genistein found in fermented soy such as tempeh encourages our sick cells to die off called apoptosis. (Wilson, 1995)

Wow! Move over animal protein! Easy to digest tempeh is found in the refrigerated section in the produce department of your local grocer. Try other types of tempeh such as three-grain, bacon, flax, barley, and oat tempeh. You will find a high-quality tempeh at Rhapsody in Cabot, Vermont.

Magazine Navy Beans

- 1 cup navy beans soaked in water for 8 hours or overnight (discard soaking water)
- 1-inch piece of soaked kombu (discard soaking water)
- 3 sprigs of thyme
- pinch of salt
- 1/2 sweet onion, minced
- 1/2 yellow, red, or orange bell pepper
- 1 carrot, minced
- 1 tablespoon sesame oil
- 2 teaspoons sweet white miso, diluted in 2 teaspoons water
- juice of one lemon
- 1 teaspoon fresh ginger juice

Place kombu on bottom of heavy pot.

Add the beans.

Add just enough water to cover plus one inch.

Bring to boil.

Allow to cook for 5 minutes and skim off the foam and discard.

Add thyme to pot.

Lower to simmer and cook with lid on for 2 1/2–3 hours.

Check the water level at 1/2-hour intervals making sure the beans stay covered. Add water just to cover if needed.

Add the salt at the end of cooking and stir to combine.

In a sauté pan, add minced vegetables to oil and sauté until tender. Turn off heat.

Add miso, lemon, and ginger to sautéed vegetables and add beans.

Allow the miso to integrate for 3 minutes. Serve warm.

This dish may be pretty enough to be in a magazine.

Chapter 9

The Festival of Vegetables

I have observed what and how people eat for decades now. A hobby of mine is people-watching. It has shown me the evidence of the source of degeneration and the deterioration of health that we face. While caring for patients in the hospital, many times I find if the patient is obese, so are the children. If the patient has mucus problems, so will other family members. Diseases run in families many times because diets run in families.

These are my suggestions (even if eating from the SAD diet). Turn off all media and have a relationship with your food. Please sit down to eat. Sitting relaxes the abdominal muscles, allowing for proper digestion. It is common to chew on the run as a nurse, a habit that was hard for me to break. In a quick moment, consider those involved in the growing, harvesting, and preparation of your food. Mindfulness fuels gratitude for the food that fuels you. Soup first if eating. Pleasant conversation if eating with others. Politics and crime accounts can be discussed at another time. For goodness' sake, chew! Avoid carbonated beverages within an hour of a meal. Carbon dioxide neutralizes stomach acid.

Stop eating when you are 80 percent full. Overeating creates lethargy, brain fog, and indigestion. Without going through the physiology of digestion, trust me on this one. Overeating is taxing, especially to liver energy, which allows the life force to flow freely within us. Have you ever felt lethargic after a holiday feast? That is a clear example of blocked liver energy. Use your digestive fire for more important work like healing or creating the next chapter of your life.

Our life-giving plant foods grow during a season for a reason. The plants that surround us are a part of our vibration. Nature is marvelous in that it provides us the foods to adapt to our environments. Each season, foods erupt from the earth in a timely manner and nourish our organs and meridians that correlate specifically to each season. It is within the master plan of nature that we eat the foods that are native to us.

Eating what is grown locally and seasonally may be the healthiest advice I can give. Tropical fruits grow in hot climates because they are cooling, allowing adaptation to the heat. Hot spices grown in the tropics raise the body's temperature to induce sweating to cool the body through evaporation. They expand our energy outward to dissipate the heat—just as root vegetables and hearty greens grow in colder climates to bring energy inward to create warmth.

When we eat the foods grown outside of our climate, our balance of energy is disturbed. It may feel like internal tightness or chaos, and we get enough of that through everyday life. Eating raw salad during a snowstorm may not be as healthy as you think. It is not seasonal, is too cooling, and can create stagnation in our energy flow. Eating locally and seasonally makes us feel at home in our bodies because we are. Local foods contain the sun, soil, and local nutrients that are a part of us. This makes local food easier to digest and absorb because it harmonizes our metabolism. When we eat cold-climate foods, it increases our metabolic rate to produce heat to adapt to the cold elements of winter. The same is true when eating tropical foods, establishing just enough energy to sustain basic living. Have you ever noticed that a simple task as a grocery purchase in the cold North takes three minutes while the same transaction in the hot South takes thirty minutes?

Eating local foods also supports our local farmers, keeps the local economy healthy, and does not use excessive fuel to ship food around the world.

We already know that food has protein, fat, and carbohydrates. However, every food also contains a specific energy from the magnetic charge of heaven and earth's influence. We see this in the way food grows. Vegetables grow in three ways.

Leaves

Leaves grow upward and outward from the ground or a tree. They create an effect of gentle expansion and relaxation in the body. They create softness in hardened areas and provide oxygenation from chlorophyll. Compare a collard green to arugula. You will notice that the collard is larger, longer, and wider. It contains more of that upward dispersing energy. The arugula is smaller and more compact and contains more downward and inward energy.

All leaves support and nourish the upper body. This is very true for women and breast health. The upward energy of a leafy green keeps energy circulating throughout the chest. Greens are a good absorbable source of calcium. Lightly steamed or blanched greens at every meal will relax the internal organs, leaving you feeling soft and calm. Try to include greens at breakfast and notice the uplifting feeling of your body and mood.

Round Ground Vegetables

This category of vegetables grows on the surface of the ground and includes broccoli, cauliflower, squash, onion, turnip, and cabbage. They resonate with and nourish the organs of digestion that are just beneath the diaphragm. These are the stomach, spleen, and pancreas. Round vegetables stabilize energy in the body and mind.

Roots

Root vegetables drill downward into the earth, and their energies are reflected in the downward organs of the body. They anchor us to the world. Enjoy a variety of root veggies such as carrot, parsnip, burdock, lotus, and daikon radish. Roots offer strength and nourishment to the colon, uterus, prostate, and lower bodily functions.

Assess your vegetable intake. Are you eating all three vegetable types in every meal or at least every day? Vegetables establish an alkaline blood quality that is vital to recover from a health condition and then maintain health thereafter.

Energy from homegrown vegetables is best. Before planting your seeds, put them in your mouth for ten minutes to allow the seeds to pick up your vibration. You'll grow food with your specific needs programmed in them. Now we are really having a relationship with our food!

> All plants have a cellulose coating that cannot be broken down by chewing. Eating raw vegetables can prevent the absorption of its nutrients. It is best to lightly steam, blanch, or press your vegetables to break down the coating. A quick blanch or steam until the vegetable turns bright in color removes this coating, allowing you to chew your way to health and happiness.

The energetics of vegetables

Leaves nourish the upper body, round vegetables nourish the middle of the body, and roots nourish the lower body. The way that I am holding the vegetables shows how they grow in the ground, and how they behave in the body. Interesting, right?

Who Stole My Roll?

- 1 large collard green
- 1/2 carrot sliced lengthwise
- 1/4 cup arugula
- 1 scallion
- 1/3 cup drained organic sauerkraut

In a pot of salted water, blanch the collard and the carrot separately.

Shear off the thick stem that runs along the back of the collard for easy rolling.

Dry and lay the collard on a sushi mat or flat surface with right side down.

Place the carrot along the widest part of the collard.

Next, place the scallion next to the carrot.

Spread the arugula and sauerkraut alongside the carrot.

Roll the collard tightly and squeeze out any excess liquid.

Slice into 1-inch bite-sized pieces.

Serve with Boss of Sauce (page 195) or Pumpkin Seed Dressing. (page 196)

> When buying organic, most vegetables do not need to be peeled. The delicate vitamins and nutrients lie just beneath and in the skin. A simple rinse or scrub with a vegetable brush will do. If your produce is not organic, go ahead and peel because pesticide residue is on the surface and penetrates into the flesh.

Not all produce needs to be organic. I follow the clean fifteen and dirty dozen rule. More than thirty-two thousand foods have been tested and categorized by the US Department of Agriculture and the Food and Drug Administration, deeming fifteen foods with the least pesticide exposure and the twelve most chemically contaminated foods. The clean fifteen is a list of foods that carry an insignificant pesticide residue:

- asparagus
- avocado
- broccoli
- cabbage
- cantaloupe
- cauliflower
- eggplant
- honeydew melon
- kiwi
- mushrooms
- onion
- papaya
- peas
- pineapple
- sweet corn

The dirty dozen is best if organic:

- apples
- celery
- cherries
- grapes
- kale
- nectarines
- peaches
- pears
- potatoes
- spinach
- strawberries
- tomatoes

The Royal Boil Salad

- 1 bunch of organic kale
- 1 cup cabbage, green, purple, or Chinese, chopped
- 1 small head of broccoli florets
- 4 radishes
- handful of snow peas
- 1 carrot, julienne

In a large pot of salted water, begin to blanch each vegetable individually and place them in a strainer to remove excess water.

Place in a bowl or on a platter.

Arrange the vegetables on top of the greens and serve with a dressing that you like.

Pumpkin seed dressing pairs well with vegetables.

Of course, any green can be used in a boiled salad, which is really a quick blanch. The chards and spinach contain a high level of oxalic acid and should be eaten only on occasion, especially if kidney stones or arthritis are problems. Cook the mildest-tasting and lightly colored vegetables first. Vary the combinations of vegetables daily and according to the seasons. Try these combinations.

- arugula/daikon/squash/leek/red cabbage
- collard greens/carrot/ onion/celery
- chopped brussels/cauliflower/red radish/scallion

Let's Act Like *Rice* | 167

The Royal Boil with Pumpkin Seed dressing

> Prepare greens by pulling off leaves, starting at the bottom, and pulling off in one quick motion. The stems will be bare. Chop the stems into little pieces and include them in the preparation. The stems are the spine of the plant and offer great strength to *your* spine. After blanching or cooking the greens, place them on a cutting board and chop while hot. Chopping after cooking the greens whole, preserves the delicate nutrients that can be lost when the surface area is smaller as when chopping before cooking.

Salad is pressed to create balance with the watery aspect of raw vegetables and removes the cellulose. It provides for easy digestion and keeps the live enzymes intact. The salt or acid used to press a salad acts as a cooking process. If you want to absorb all the goodness that nature has to offer, do not eat plants in the raw. Any vegetable suitable for a salad can be pressed. Any acid or salt can be used as an extractor. Try miso, fresh lemon juice, umeboshi vinegar, or shoyu. Pressing is a way of cooking vegetables without applying heat. The elements of time, pressure, and salt balance the energy of raw vegetables. This technique can be used for any vegetable or combination of vegetables and greens for greater balance of food energetics. Add more pressing time for thicker vegetables.

I learned this technique at the Kushi Institute, the school that taught me the greatest knowledge of life. Before leaving, I found a rock there that had beautiful color and weight. I decided that that rock would be my pressing rock and brought it home. I cleaned it and cleared it with my crystals, and it sits on my kitchen shelf as a beacon of macrobiotic wisdom. As I remember that day and share the description of my rock with you, I find myself getting choked up.

My Pressing Rock

Undressed Pressed Salad

- 1 cup Chinese cabbage, finely chopped
- 1 cup bitter green, such as mustard green, radish green, dandelion green, or arugula
- 1 carrot, grated or shredded
- 3 radishes, thinly sliced
- 1 stalk celery, finely sliced
- 1/4 small red onion, sliced into thin half moons
- 1/2 green apple, thinly sliced
- 1 teaspoon salt
- 2 tablespoons freshly squeezed lemon juice

Combine first 7 ingredients in a large bowl.

Sprinkle salt and lemon juice into veggies.

Massage the salt and lemon juice into the veggies with your fingers. The strength of your hand will be translated into the strength of the dish.

Place a plate inside the bowl.

Set a weight on top or use a pickle press.

Press for 30–60 minutes.

Drain liquid and serve. (Sometimes I leave the pressed liquid in the bottom of the bowl.) It has a high oxygen content.

This is delicious enough that dressing is not needed.

Pressed Salad in Pickle Press

Hail to Kale

- 1 head organic kale or other hearty green, finely chopped
- 1 organic carrot, grated
- 1 small organic daikon radish, thinly sliced
- 1 organic red onion, sliced very thin
- 1/2 teaspoon unrefined sea salt

Add vegetables to salad bowl.

Sprinkle salt onto salad and massage into vegetables. Continue to rub and toss the salad until it begins to wilt.

Place a small plate inside the bowl with a weight on top. A pickle press can also be used.

Allow vegetables to press for 1–2 hours.

Drain off liquid and serve salad as is or drizzle with a dressing of your choice.

> Kale contains goitrogens, which can negatively affect the thyroid when eaten raw. Blanching, steaming, pressing, baking, or stir-frying can remedy this. Use caution when using raw kale in a smoothie.

Hump Day Greens

- 1/4 cup organic bulgur wheat
- 1/2 cup boiling water
- pinch of salt
- 1 tablespoon extra-virgin olive oil
- 1 small sweet onion, chopped
- 4 cups greens—collards, kale, mustard greens—chopped

Pour the boiling water over the bulgur wheat in a bowl.

Stir in the salt and cover the bowl, allowing the bulgur to steam.

Let steep for 20 minutes or until the wheat is soft.

Sauté onion in oil in a skillet until onions become caramelized.

Add a pinch of salt to the onions.

Add greens to the skillet and continue to sauté until greens turn bright green.

Add a pinch of salt to the greens.

Add softened bulgur wheat to the greens and mix together in the skillet.

Serve as a side dish.

> My friend's mom came from Syria and taught me the cooking and culture of the Middle East. She told me many stories of riding camels through town just as we drive cars. This recipe is hers. She used spinach in the dish and called the dish *Bitatho*.

Let's Act Like Rice | 173

Bitatho

Zero Point Cucumber Salad

If you are a Weight Watcher, you will find that many of my recipes are zero points—just as this one is. Enjoy!

- 4 organic baby or pickling cucumbers to equal 2 cups
- 3-inch piece of soaked and chopped wakame to total 1/4 cup
- 2 tablespoons fresh dill, finely minced
- 1/4 cup organic rice vinegar
- pinch of salt
- splash of organic mirin (without sugar or chemicals)

Place cucumbers and all ingredients in a bowl.

Toss to combine.

Serve as a refreshing side dish.

Zero Point Cucumber Salad

Steamed Greens with Envy

- 4 collard green leaves
- 4 kale leaves
- 4 cabbage leaves
- pinch of salt

Place whole leaves in a steamer with salt.

Place steamer over boiling water.

Steam until the leaves turn bright green, approximately 5 minutes.

Turn off heat.

Turn hot greens onto a cutting board and cut into bite-sized pieces.

A squeeze of fresh lemon or the flavor of umeboshi will heighten this dish. Choose a variety of greens and mix them up. Have you ever tried turnip greens, mustard greens, dandelion greens, watercress, or purple cabbage?

Steamed, blanched, or pressed greens are best eaten with every meal, including breakfast. Greens are very alkalizing to the blood and create moisture with the high oxygen content of the leaf. Greens cleanse and hydrate the skin. Soon, you will glow with radiance.

Steamed Kale, Collards, and Cabbage

Let's Act Like Rice | 177

Steamed greens with toasted pumpkin seeds

Flip-Flops and Carrot Tops

- 2 cups carrot tops, washed and chopped
- 1/4 cup sesame seeds, roasted
- 1 teaspoon shoyu or a pinch of salt

Blanch the carrot tops in a pot with 1/4-inch water and the salt or shoyu. Carrot tops are delicate and turn bright green quickly.

Remove from pot and drain.

Rinse sesame seeds in a strainer, place into a hot cast-iron pan or skillet. Toss them around and keep them moving. They will toast quickly and give a nutty fragrance.

Sprinkle carrot tops with seeds.

The tops of carrots are high in chlorophyll and are amazing at cleansing the body. The taste is bitter, which is an important flavor for heart health. Carrot tops are abundant in summertime when heart energy is at its fullest. So, put on your flip-flops and eat your carrot tops.

Flip-Flops and Carrot Tops

Boasted Roasted Vegetables

- large sweet potato, chopped into small pieces or roll cut
- 2 carrots, cut the same size as potato
- 1/2 red onion, cut into half moons
- 1 cup chopped broccoli stem (reserve the florets for another dish)
- 1/4 cup kalamata olives, pitted
- 1 tablespoon sesame oil
- 1 tablespoon shoyu
- 1/2 cup water
- 1/3 cup plain mochi, grated

Preheat oven to 350 degrees.

Mix all ingredients in a baking dish.

Bake uncovered for 30–40 minutes (cooking time will depend on the size of the vegetables).

Stir the vegetables halfway through cooking time. The mochi produces a gravy-like sauce.

The vegetables can vary according to the season. Try brussels sprouts, squash, fennel, and string beans.

Jammin' Onion Jam

- 6 large Vidalia onions
- 1–2 tablespoons extra-virgin olive oil
- 1 teaspoon salt

Add all ingredients into a heavy stock pot.

On high heat, begin to sizzle the onions in oil.

Stir to keep the onions moving.

Keep them on high until they begin to caramelize.

Continue stirring and turn heat to medium-low to prevent burning.

After 30 minutes, the onions will soften and begin to break down. Continue cooking until the onions no longer hold their shape.

Stir every few minutes. When the onions become soft mush, they are done. This can take an hour or so.

Turn off heat and allow to cool.

Onion jam can be enjoyed on crackers or bread or as a topping on grains.

Mimi's Nishimi

- 1 strip of kombu, soaked in water until soft and then drained
- 1 cup daikon, sliced
- 1 cup carrot, cut into rounds
- 1 cup rutabaga or turnip, chopped
- 1 small sweet onion, quartered
- 1 cup winter squash or sweet potato, cubed
- a few small pinches of salt
- 1–2 tablespoons shoyu

Keep the size of vegetables the same to assure even cooking. Place kombu on bottom of a heavy pot and layer vegetables on top.

Add enough water to fill pot to 1/2 inch (ironically, Nishimi means waterless cooking).

Add salt, cover, and bring to a boil.

Lower heat and simmer for 30 minutes or until vegetables are fork tender. Add water if needed. Sprinkle shoyu over Nishimi and continue cooking 5 more minutes for vegetables to absorb shoyu and strengthen the dish.

Turn heat off.

Mix vegetables with any remaining liquid and serve.

Nishimi can made with any combination of root and round vegetables. Cooking time is dependent on the thickness of the vegetables. Vary the veggies according to the seasons.

My granddaughter pronounced my name as Mimi as she was learning to talk. So, Mimi it is. (I was going for Pretty Grammy!)

Nishimi Before Cooking

Tic-Tac-Daikon

This dish is also known as *furofuki* in Japanese culture, which is where macrobiotics originated. If you are a foodie like me, impress your friends with a dish they most likely have never eaten before.

- 2 large daikon radishes
- 2 celery stalks, sliced longwise in half
- pinch of salt
- 1/4 cup mirin
- 1 tablespoon shoyu

Topping

- 2 tablespoons barley miso
- 2 tablespoons brown rice syrup
- 1 lemon, juiced and zested
- 1 teaspoon Dijon mustard
- 1 scallion, sheared into thin slivers as a garnish

Slice the daikon in large 1-inch rounds or diagonals.

Place the daikon in single layer in a pot to keep its shape. Add enough water to half cover the daikon. Sprinkle radish with mirin, shoyu, and salt. Cook in batches if needed.

With lid on, bring to a boil.

Reduce the flame to medium.

Cook daikon approximately 20–30 minutes or until fork tender.

Remove from pot and add the celery to the remaining liquid and simmer a few minutes.

Place the topping ingredients into a saucepan and heat to warm.

Arrange the celery on a serving platter in a tic-tac-toe design.

Place the daikon within the lines of the celery.

Dollop each daikon round with the topping.

Garnish with scallion.

Tic Tac Daikon

Daikon is a versatile vegetable that can be seasoned while cooking with a teaspoon of mirin, white miso, ginger, or onion juice to change it up.

Daikon is a powerful root vegetable that offers great nutrition and energy. It breaks down animal fat and protein, which is why we see it served with sushi. When transitioning to a plant-based diet, daikon helps discharge the animals we have eaten in the past. Its high in vitamin C for a strong immune system and is anti-inflammatory. It has a diuretic and expectorant effect. Its juice is a digestive aid. Daikon is full of antioxidants that prevent cancer and reverse the action of free radicals. This dish contains 150 milligrams of calcium, which makes our bones and blood happy. The energy of this dish helps eliminate stagnation of chi and physical tightness. It has a relaxing effect on digestion due to its dissolving power.

In Cahoots with Roots

Roots drill their way into the earth and bring that strengthening downward energy into our downward body parts (beneath the belly button). This dish, known as *kinpira*, brings vitality to all the pelvic organs, particularly the colon. Roots draw deep earth energy into them and release it into us in a delicious way. This dish does just that.

- 1 tablespoon toasted sesame oil
- 1 cup burdock root, matchstick cut
- 1 cup carrot, matchstick cut
- splash of shoyu to taste
- 1 tablespoon toasted sesame seeds

Heat oil in a skillet on high heat and sauté the burdock until it begins to soften.

Add carrots on top of burdock—but do not mix them together.

Add 1/2 cup water and quickly apply the lid. The veggies will steam.

Reduce heat to low and simmer until carrots begin to soften.

Add the shoyu and continue cooking until vegetables are perfectly soft. Not crunchy, not mushy. Just right.

Remove from heat.

Serve topped with toasted sesame seeds.

Other roots to include in this dish are parsnips and lotus root if desired. A squeeze of fresh ginger juice makes this dish warming on a cold day.

Kinpira with Lotus Root

🌾 Burdock root is a gnarly branch-like root that gives a dish a rich sweetness. If you have ever walked through a meadow and found spikey prickers stuck to your clothing, you found burdock root! Do not peel burdock. Simply rinse or wash with a vegetable brush. Burdock has many profound health benefits. It amazingly cleanses the blood of toxins as it strengthens kidney function, according to a 2011 study. The study also includes evidence of a potent inhibitory effect on the growth of pancreatic cancer (Yuk-Shing Chan, 2011). It contains many antioxidants, including a significant amount of vitamins C and E, as well as quercetin, luteolin, and phenolic acids, which all have cancer-protective properties. Other studies have proven burdock to be an aphrodisiac (Cao Jian Feng, 2012).

Well, that one I am not sure of, but you can be the judge. Because of its anti-inflammatory and antibacterial properties, burdock has been used for many years in treating acne, psoriasis, and eczema. It is also a natural diuretic and assists the liver in detoxifying and regulating hormones. It can be cooked or steeped as a tea, powder, or extract.

Because it grows deep in the ground, it brings energy deep into the body and focus to the mind and improves cognitive function. I have seen children with scattered thinking and weak attention flourish when including burdock in their diet. Burdock is so strong that it will split a rock in half if it is in the path of its growth! That is one strong root!

I once suggested that the public city school board replace the doughnuts and fruit juice they serve to the children before standardized tests with burdock. They are still laughing at me!

Burdock

High on Stir Fry

- 2 tablespoons toasted sesame oil
- 1 carrot, cut into thin coins or diagonals. If you're skilled with a knife, try ribbons or flower cut.
- 1 lotus root, cut into thin slices that show its beautiful design
- 1 sweet onion, sliced into half moons
- 1 head broccoli, cut into small florets
- 5 leaves of green, Napa, Chinese, or savoy cabbage, cut into bite-sized pieces
- 4 dried shiitake mushrooms, soaked in 3/4 cup water to soften, remove, and discard the stems and chop. Reserve the water.
- few pinches of salt
- 2 tablespoons each of shoyu, brown rice vinegar, freshly grated ginger juice
- 1/2 cup organic apple juice
- 2 tablespoons kudzu
- chopped scallion to garnish

Over medium-high heat, add oil, carrot, lotus, onion, broccoli, cabbage, shiitake, and salt into a skillet or wok. Sauté until vegetables become crunch tender (approximately 10–15 minutes).

Let us not be too serious. Sautéing vegetables is fun!

Add shoyu, vinegar, ginger juice, and apple juice.

Dissolve kudzu in the reserved shiitake water.

Push the vegetables to the sides of the pan, creating a hole in the center.

Add diluted kudzu to the center while constantly stirring. Kudzu will thicken as it heats.

Incorporate all the vegetables in the thickened sauce.

Remove from heat and garnish with scallion.

Let's Act Like Rice | 189

High on Stir Fry on a bed of brown rice

The Power of Cauliflower

- 1 head each cauliflower and broccoli, washed and cut into bite-sized florets
- 1 cup rinsed and dried pea shoots

Dressing

- 1/2 cup pan-toasted sesame seeds
- 1 tablespoon umeboshi paste
- 1/2 cup water
- 2 tablespoons brown rice vinegar or lemon juice

Steam or blanch vegetables in lightly salted water until crunchy tender or desired softness.

Place pea shoots on a serving dish and top with cooked vegetables.

Add the rest of the ingredients into a jar and shake it up!

Pour the seed mixture on top of the entire dish of vegetables.

> Cauliflower is a cruciferous vegetable that brings the body fiber, vitamins, antioxidants, and phytonutrients. It contains choline, which is a member of the vitamin B family. Choline is important for learning, memory, and all higher brain functions. Energetically, it resonates with the brain and the lungs.

Let's Act Like *Rice* | 191

The Power of Cauliflower

Chapter 10

The Blessings of Dressings

Donna's Famous Salad Dressing

Well, here it is, folks: the dressing that people know me by.

Person 1: Do you know Donna?
Person 2: Yes. She is the lady who makes that special salad dressing.

This is what I am asked to bring anytime I attend an event or party. I never thought I would reveal my secret, but it's out of the bag now.

- 1 cup exceptionally fine organic extra-virgin olive oil
- (To test a good olive oil, sip the oil and aerate it in your mouth. It should have a mild burn in the back of your taste buds.)
- 1/2 cup flavored natural vinegar
- In spring and summer, I macerate raspberries or other fruits into a plain organic rice vinegar to create new flavors. In fall and winter, I add figs and dried or fresh herbs.
- 1/4 cup other organic vinegar, such as white wine vinegar, a balsamic vinegar, or apple

- cider vinegar. It all depends on your mood.
- the juice of one lemon
- (Go nuts when Meyer lemons are in season!)
- 1 tablespoon brown rice syrup
- 2 teaspoons Dijon mustard
- 1–2 garlic cloves, grated
- 1–2 tablespoon onion juice, freshly grated
- 1/2 teaspoon dried basil
- 1/2 teaspoon dried oregano
- 1/2 teaspoon dried parsley
- 1/2 teaspoon salt

Add all ingredients to a glass bottle or jar and shake it up.

For aesthetics and extra flavor, add a visual to the bottle such as a sprig of thyme, basil, dill, or parsley.

Stays fresh for 1–2 weeks in refrigerator.

As you can see, there are many variables. I never make the same dressing twice. The season, the event, and my intuition guide me to mix it up as needed—and so will you. The key is to combine two different vinegars and good quality oil.

Add this or any dressing to a pretty bottle with a bow and give it as a gift. Most people love a homemade dressing because homemade requires time-something we never seem to have enough of. This is a beautiful way of gifting your love.

Donna's Dressing

Donna's Dressing

The Boss of Sauce

- 1/2 cup lemon juice
- 1 heaping tablespoon Dijon mustard
- 1 teaspoon shoyu
- 1 teaspoon kudzu

Place lemon juice, mustard, and shoyu in a small saucepan and heat to simmer.

Dilute kudzu in 1 tablespoon cold water to remove the lumps.

Begin stirring lemon mixture while whisking in kudzu into pot.

Continue to whisk until translucent and thickened.

Serve warm or at room temperature.

Top grain or vegetables with this sauce.

Miso Almond Sauce

- 4 tablespoons sweet white or barley miso
- 6 tablespoons almond butter
- 1 1/2 cups boiling water

Mix the miso and almond butter together in a glass bowl with half of the water into a pasty slurry.

Add remaining water and mix thoroughly.

Serve on vegetables, grain, or steamed tofu—or stir into hot soba noodles.

Pumpkin Seed Dressing

- 1 cup pumpkin seeds, toasted
- 2 tablespoons umeboshi paste
- handful of fresh flat leaf parsley, chopped
- 3–4 chopped scallions

In a strainer, rinse seeds and toss into a hot cast-iron pan or skillet. Toss the seeds around with a wooden utensil. As they toast, a delicious fragrance is released—and soon everybody enters the kitchen to see what's going on!

They are done toasting when they begin to pop and turn a golden-brown color.

While still hot, grind them into a paste in a suribachi, food processer, or blender.

Add the paste, parsley, and scallion.

Add enough water for desired consistency.

Adjust to taste.

Pumpkin Seed Dressing

Bellini Tahini Dressing

- 1/2 cup tahini
- 1/4 cup lime juice
- 1/4 cup minced herb of your choice: basil, cilantro, dill, scallion
- 2 tablespoons of champagne vinegar

Mix all ingredients in a jar.

Avocado Salado

- 1 ripe organic avocado, peeled and pitted
- 2 tablespoons extra-virgin olive oil
- 1/2 cup organic white balsamic vinegar
- 1/2 cup freshly squeezed lemon juice
- 1 teaspoon dried basil or 5 leaves chopped fresh basil
- 1 heaping teaspoon sweet white miso

Combine all ingredients in a suribachi or mash with a fork or potato masher until desired consistency.

Avocado Salado

Very Strawberry Dressing

- 1 pint farm fresh strawberries
- 1/2 cup organic balsamic vinegar
- 1/2 cup organic apple juice
- 1 tablespoon shoyu

Grind, mash, or blend into a rich and creamy topping to any salad or vegetable.

Vampire's Dressing

- 4–5 cloves roasted garlic
- 1/2 cup extra-virgin olive oil
- 1/2 cup rice vinegar
- juice of 1 lemon
- 1-inch piece of fresh ginger
- 1/8 teaspoon salt

Grind all ingredients together in a grinding bowl or add all ingredients to a blender and blend until smooth.

> To roast garlic in a skillet or cast-iron pan, heat a pan on high heat and add garlic with skin intact. When browning begins, flip garlic so it browns evenly. Allow to cool and peel.

No Messing with This Dressing

- 2 cups flat leaf parsley leaves
- 3 scallions
- 1/3 cup sesame or olive oil
- 3 tablespoons umeboshi paste
- 1 cup water

Add all ingredients into a grinding bowl or blender.

No Messing Dressing and Tofu Fetta is Betta

Dreamy Tahini Sauce

- 1/2 cup tahini
- 2 tablespoons sweet white miso
- 1/2 cup water

Mix tahini, miso, and water together.

Use this sauce to top grain or noodles as a little something extra.

The addition of freshly squeezed lemon juice or a splash of brown rice vinegar is a compliment to this dressing. Including the flavor of onion such as a minced scallion or shallot is also delicious.

The Creamy Almond

- 1/4 cup almond butter
- juice of 1 lime
- 1 tablespoon brown rice vinegar
- pinch of salt
- 1/2 teaspoon of freshly grated ginger juice

Mix ingredients together with enough water for the desired consistency.

Creamy Dreamy Dressing

- 2/3 cup unsweetened almond milk
- 1 tablespoon lemon juice
- 1 cup raw cashews, soaked overnight or simmered for 15 minutes
- zest of one lemon
- 1 garlic clove, peeled
- 1/2 teaspoon salt
- 1 tablespoon grated onion
- 2 tablespoons brown rice vinegar
- 1 tablespoon maple syrup

Add lemon juice to almond milk and let sit a few minutes. The combination of milk and acid mimics buttermilk.

Drain the cashews and place them in a blender or grinding bowl.

Add almond milk/lemon juice, zest, garlic, salt, onion, vinegar, and syrup.

Blend until creamy.

A handful of fresh herbs, such as scallions, parsley, dill, or cilantro, makes a unique flavor and adds color to the dressing if desired.

Creamy Dreamy Dressing

Supreme Sour Cream

- 1 package organic firm tofu
- 4 tablespoons fresh lemon juice
- 2 tablespoons umeboshi vinegar
- 1 tablespoon apple cider vinegar
- 1 pan-roasted clove of garlic
- ½ teaspoon powdered mustard
- 1 tablespoon brown rice syrup
- 2 tablespoons sesame oil or extra-virgin olive oil

Boil or steam tofu for 20 minutes to balance the cold energies of the tofu.

When cooled, add tofu and other ingredients and blend until smooth.

Lasts one week refrigerated.

This recipe is the backdrop to many other creamy dressings.

The addition of freshly grated horseradish or red onion, avocado, or minced herbs will bring sour cream to new heights.

Supreme Sour Cream

Lemon Walnut Dunk

- 1/4 cup walnuts
- 1/2 cup brown rice syrup
- 2 tablespoons water
- Juice of a 1/2 lemon

Rinse walnuts in a colander and then transfer to a hot skillet. Shake the pan back and forth to prevent the nuts from sticking. Remove the pan from the heat when they become toasted brown and release a nutty fragrance.

Add the rice syrup, water, and nuts to the hot skillet and stir together. The residual heat in the skillet is all that is needed to heat the dunk.

Add the lemon juice and stir to combine.

Whenever my kids dipped food, they called it *dunk*. So be it.

Trick or Treat Beet Dressing

- 2 tablespoons brown rice vinegar
- 1 tablespoon fresh lemon juice
- 1 teaspoon Dijon mustard
- 1 tablespoon grated onion
- 4 cooked red beets
- 1/4 cup extra-virgin olive oil

Blend together until smooth.

Makes for a bloody-appearing salad or veggie-dipping sauce for Halloween. Yup! I have worked in the intensive care unit far too long!

Trick or Treat Beet Dressing

Chapter 11

In a Pickle Now!

The incorporation of fermentation in the diet is greatly beneficial if not crucial to vibrant health. It creates the biome, feeds the biome, and on all accounts, makes us happy. One tablespoon per day is all that is needed. I agree that it is much easier to buy store-bought pickles, but after reading the ingredient list on many store-bought brands, you may reconsider and choose to make homemade pickles for your health's sake. They are inexpensive and easy to make, and the reward is immense. Fermenting vegetables can be a creative outlet by trying new vegetables and pickling agents. Soon you will be naming your own pickles!

My Own Biome Pickles

- 1/2 teaspoon sea salt
- 2 cups green cabbage, shredded
- 1/2 cup purple cabbage, shredded
- 2 carrots, shredded
- 1/2 cup cauliflower, chopped small

Sprinkle salt over the vegetables in a bowl. Massage the salt into the vegetables. The vegetables will release some of their liquid.

Mix the next six ingredients together as a marinade.

- 2 tablespoons organic brown rice vinegar
- 2 tablespoons organic lemon juice
- 1 tablespoon organic mirin
- 2 teaspoons organic white miso
- 1 teaspoon grated ginger
- 1 teaspoon ground mustard

Pour the marinade over the vegetables.

Pack the vegetables and marinade into a mason jar, being sure the vegetables are completely covered in the liquid. A full leaf of cabbage can be placed at the top of the jar if needed to keep the vegetables submerged. A clean rock can also be used.

Cover the mouth of the jar with a cheesecloth and secure with an elastic.

Marinate vegetables for at least twenty-four hours at room temperature. The longer they sit at room temperature, the stronger the fermentation.

After twenty-four hours, replace the cheesecloth with a lid.

Refrigerate.

Stays fresh for one week. Tip the jar upside down every couple of days to keep the vegetables moist. If the flavor becomes too strong, simply rinse with water.

My Own Biome Pickle

Sauerkraut

- 1 white cabbage, washed, cored, and very finely shredded (reserve one full crispy leaf)
- 1 1/2 tablespoons natural salt

Place the cabbage in a bowl and sprinkle with salt.

Massage the salt into the cabbage until the cabbage becomes wilted with its own juices.

Pack the cabbage and its juices into a mason jar. Packing tightly ensures that air is not trapped inside the jar.

Lay the full cabbage leaf over the top of the container, submerging the cabbage into the jar.

Apply the lid loosely.

Leave on the counter at room temperature for 2 weeks.

Check your sauerkraut frequently for signs of fermentation. You may find foam or gas bubbles. You may wipe away any foam or mold. It is perfectly safe.

After 2 weeks, open the jar and taste. If it is to your liking, place it in the refrigerator. If you prefer a stronger product, continue the fermentation process and check on it daily.

Lasts for one month refrigerated, but most likely, it will be eaten by then.

Adding other ingredients to your sauerkraut makes for unique flavors. Here are a few additions that I have tried: juniper berries, caraway seeds, celery seeds, hijiki, and garlic.

Making sauerkraut is creating a new life. I find it exciting to watch my baby in the jar transform from a raw vegetable to a live food. Sometimes I name it and talk to it. That only proves how a healthy gut makes for a happy mind. Fermented cabbage is prebiotic, probiotic, and psychobiotic. Let's get happy!

Basic Brine

- 2 cups water
- 1 tablespoon salt

Wash, chop, and prepare any vegetable of your liking.

Place vegetables in a glass jar.

Add brine to vegetables.

Cover the jar with cheesecloth and secure with an elastic.

Leave on countertop for twenty-four hours at room temperature.

Replace cheesecloth with lid.

Refrigerate.

Stays fresh for one week.

I Will Shoyu Pickles

- 1/4 cup shoyu
- 3/4 cups water
- 1 cup thinly sliced vegetables (radishes, broccoli stems, cauliflower, carrots, or my favorite— rutabaga rounds)

Slice one or a combination of vegetables thinly and place in a jar.

Add water and shoyu, making sure that the vegetables are covered.

Choose a jar that fits vegetables and liquid without space at the top. You may weigh down the vegetables in the jar with a cabbage leaf or other green if needed. Place the lid on the jar and shake to distribute shoyu evenly.

Remove lid and cover jar with a piece of cheesecloth.

Secure with a rubber band.

Let sit at room temperature for twenty-four hours.

Replace cheesecloth with the lid and refrigerate for another twenty-four hours. Your pickles are now ready to enjoy.

Your gut will thank you.

They will last for 1 week refrigerated.

If they become too salty, just give them a little rinse.

This brine can be reused.

Chapter 12

The Notion That the Potion Is in the Ocean

Minerals are the most important element to health. Our blood is built on the foundation of minerals. The proportion of proteins, carbohydrates, water, and micronutrients is dependent on the amount and quality of mineralized blood. Every biological function of the human body relies on adequate levels of minerals.

People are always asking me where I get my calcium. My answer? If the cow gets its calcium from grass and builds a bone structure weighing seven hundred pounds—then so do I!

I do not rely on dairy for an important mineral such as calcium. When eating a plant-based macrobiotic diet, absorbable calcium comes from many sources. In my thirty-year experience of helping those regain their health with macrobiotics, the removal of dairy has alleviated the symptoms of allergies, autoimmune diseases, cystic acne, polycystic ovaries, sinusitis, asthma, ear infections, IBS, respiratory infections, a variety of hormone-related cancers, myelin sheath diseases, and much more.

Eliminating dairy decreases your saturated fat intake, thus reducing the risk of dementia, heart disease, and type 2 diabetes. These are conditions that we have control over that bring unhappiness into our lives. It has affected every health condition I have witnessed. My conclusion? Dairy is the most harmful ingredient to our health. It creates an acidic condition in the body, begins the process of inflammation, and produces mucus in and around the organs. Mucus is the medium that viruses attach to in the respiratory tract, particularly coronaviruses. Maybe it should come with a warning label.

Isn't it interesting that American women consume large amounts of dairy, particularly yogurt, and have one of the highest rates of osteoporosis (Scientists link drinking milk with Osteoporosis, 2018)?

In fact, bone degeneration is so common that more than ten million Americans have weak and thinning bones. That is 32 percent of the population. It is a popular topic over coffee with postmenopausal women. Let us change that conversation.

Sea vegetables offer high quality minerals to the diet. In fact, sea vegetables contain ten to twenty times the minerals and vitamins than land vegetables. The minerals are in chelated form, which makes them better absorbed. Sea vegetables offer a rich banquet of minerals and nutrients such as calcium, vitamin C, B, D, E, K, iodine, iron, magnesium, manganese, melatonin, phosphorus, polymers, potassium, protein, selenium, sodium, sterols, electrolytes, omega fatty acids, fiber, and folate.

How amazing is the nutrient value from the ocean? There are more than six thousand species of edible seaweeds. Studies show that sea vegetables are antiviral, which is important to know since I am writing this during the COVID-19 pandemic, neuroprotective, and prevent cancer growth. Their lignan content is a strong breast cancer protector. Umami, considered the fifth flavor, is brought about in sea vegetables through different cooking styles. A steady intake of minerals from the ocean creates a flexible mind and attitude. If those around you are telling you that you are stubborn and inflexible, serve up a helping of seaweed!

The quality of sea vegetables is as important as the quality of other foods we eat. To ensure safety, choose products from producers you trust. I use sea vegetables by Mitoku and Eden. They grow their greens in pristine waters and check for radiation exposure. They hold higher standards than what is regulated. Maine Seaweed is also a trusted brand. Sea vegetables are concentrated minerals. They are purchased dry and reconstituted before cooking. They will expand considerably when rehydrated. Sea greens can be used in recipes from smoothies to desserts.

Websites

- Eden.com
- Mitoku.com
- Theseaweedman.com

Hijiki

Grows 6–7 feet deep in the ocean and looks like a pine bush. Hijiki is the medicine of the sea. Its high calcium content exceeds dairy and is necessary for bone health. Its energetic force nourishes the lungs and large intestine. Want beautiful skin, hair, and nails? Toss a bit of hijiki in your soup, salad, or stir-fry. Hijiki is the mineral hero, being exceptional in calcium, iron, iodine, fiber, potassium, B vitamins, magnesium, and zinc. Its natural balance of calcium and magnesium can relax those nasty nighttime leg cramps and is essential for restful sleep. Hijiki is the strongest-tasting vegetable with the highest mineral content. It is said that a diet rich in hijiki will reverse gray hair back to its original color.

Hijiki requires thirty minutes of cooking time.

Kombu

Kombu (kelp) is high in glutamic acid and is used as a natural MSG and food enhancer. A postage-sized piece of soaked kombu cooked with beans, grains, and vegetables will impart flavor, aid in digestion, and diminish intestinal gas. Kombu helps break down the indigestible carbohydrates that create gas after consuming beans. Studies show that kombu assists the regression of tumors and cysts. The alginic acid found in kombu is like pectin and binds to heavy metals for excretion and is also an ingredient in many antacids.

Kombu lowers cholesterol and relieves minor water retention. It is used as a macrobiotic remedy for many conditions, including hypertension and goiter. Sea vegetables mineralize and alkalize the blood, and kombu is royalty here. It is high in calcium, iron, iodine, and vitamins B and C. Kombu is an important ingredient in making soup stocks. When cooking with kombu, soak it in a small amount of water to reconstitute, discard the water, and add the kombu to the pot. Remove the kombu from the pot after cooking, chop it up, and return it to the pot.

Wakame

This quick-cooking vegetable which is thinner than kombu. You may have eaten wakame in miso soup. It makes a nice addition to any salad. It has anti-pyloric properties that are used in the prevention and treatment of gastric ulcers. Wakame decreases bodily heat in an overheated liver condition.

Wakame is coated with a white powder that is a natural salt that softens hard growths such as the calcifications of arteriosclerosis. Its mineral content is beneficial to the pituitary and thyroid, and it is high in calcium, iron, vitamin A, potassium, and iodine. Both kombu and wakame discharge heavy metals and radioactivity from the body. Wakame harvested from Pacific waters has a peaceful energy, but the Atlantic waters are more active, creating a stronger vegetable. Always discard wakame's soaking water since it is very high in magnesium. Avoid the wakame seaweed salad found in Asian restaurants and delis because it is laden with sugar.

Nori

These thin dried sheets are commonly used to roll sushi. Cut up the nori sheets as a topping to grain or as a healthy snack. It contains vitamin A, which is vital for eye health and the prevention of night blindness. Nori is high in docosahexaenoic acid (DHA), which is an important omega-3 fatty acid. Spell nori backward to find its strength. Some nori has been found to contain vitamin B12. Its omega oil makes this seaweed strengthening to the overall health of the cardiovascular system.

Dulse

This dried alga can be eaten raw as a snack, in a salad, as a garnish, or cooked in a recipe. It adds a delightful pink color to the dish. Dulse has been used in the treatment of high blood pressure due to its potassium properties. It is imbued with beta-carotene for eyesight and contains four times the amount of iron as spinach. The minerals in dulse support the nervous system and thyroid. What a treat!

Agar

This tasteless extract from seaweed is purchased as flakes, bars, or powder and is used as a thickener to make aspic or gelatin. It dissolves in hot liquid in five to ten minutes. Agar is used as a thickener since it is the starch from the red sea algae seaweed. It contains no calories, sugar, carbohydrate, fat, or gluten, but it is a good source of fiber, calcium, and iron. It is used in the macrobiotic diet to improve digestion and detoxify the blood. It absorbs bile, which can lower cholesterol. Agar has a cooling and a mild laxative effect as well as anti-inflammatory properties.

Arame

Arame has a milder character than hijiki, a substantial texture, and fewer minerals. Mannitol, a noncaloric sugar found in arame, gives a slight sweet flavor to any dish, and its sweet taste nourishes the stomach, spleen, and pancreas. Including arame in your diet will help regulate your blood sugar. There is no need to soak arame because it is precooked.

- An average serving of hijiki contains 1400 milligrams of calcium.
- An average serving of kombu contains 710 milligrams of calcium.
- An average serving of arame contains 790 milligrams of calcium.
- An average cup of whole milk contains 305 milligrams of calcium and seven grams of casein.
- A cup of plain yogurt contains 274 milligrams calcium and 8.5 grams of casein.
- Greek yogurt is almost purely casein.
- Tofu, beans, greens, and sesame seeds will also prevent bone fractures by boosting calcium.

Get your flippers on—and let's dive in!

Treasures at Sea

- 1/2 cup sweet onion, chopped
- 1 tablespoon sesame oil
- 1 cup dried hijiki. Rinse and discard water several times. Soak in enough water to cover until soft. Discard soaking water.
- 1/2 cup organic apple juice
- 1 cup carrot, minced
- 1 cup fresh or frozen organic corn
- Brown rice syrup to taste (optional)
- 1 tablespoon toasted sesame seeds
- Fresh herb or scallion for garnish

Heat a skillet over medium heat and sauté onion in oil. Water sauté if avoiding oil.

Add hijiki, juice, and carrot.

Cover the skillet with lid and lower heat to low.

Cook 20 minutes or until vegetables are soft.

Add corn and syrup and heat through.

Remove from heat.

Top with sesame seeds.

Serve with fresh garnish.

I suggest using the syrup when cooking for children. The sweeter the dish, the more likely they are to eat it.

Treasures at Sea without corn

> 🌾 Sesame seeds provide polyunsaturated fat that is high in omega fatty acids. Sesame oil is recommended for year-round cooking. Sesame oil is delicious and makes for a nice massage oil. Sesame seeds come roasted or plain and can be crushed to make tahini or gomasio. Tan or black varieties are available as well as hulled and unlulled. It is best when refrigerated to prevent rancidity. Sesame seeds contain 88 milligrams of calcium per tablespoon! Woo hoo! They are also rich in iron (iron stores for improved blood quality and strong hemoglobin), magnesium (decreases spasms as in asthma or migraine), manganese, copper (aids in reducing inflammation as in rheumatoid arthritis), vitamin B1, thiamin, vitamin E, and zinc (reduces osteoporosis together with calcium and lowers blood pressure) Sesame seeds also contain lignans such as sesamin and sesamolin, which fight cancer. Keep them on your kitchen counter and sprinkle them freely.

The Story of Nori

Nori is made by shredding, cooking, and rack-drying seaweed, which is the same process that the Japanese use for papermaking. So, sushi was born.

- 1 cup cooked short grain brown rice
- 1 teaspoon brown rice vinegar
- 1 teaspoon mirin
- 1 package toasted nori
- 1 teaspoon umeboshi paste
- 1 carrot-cut into long strips and blanched
- 1 scallion
- 1 zucchini, sliced lengthwise and grilled or lightly pan-fried

Maki Roll

Mix vinegar and mirin into rice.

Line a sheet of nori on a sushi mat—bright side down.

Have a bowl of water next to you. Moisten your hands and press a handful of the rice on to the nori sheet.

Leave a 2-inch margin at the top of the nori and 1 inch at the bottom.

Spread a bit of the paste along the lower edge, lengthwise.

Arrange the carrot, scallion, and zucchini next to the paste.

Wet your fingers and apply moisture to the top of the nori roll. This is like the glue of an envelope.

Hold the vegetables in place while lifting the sushi mat and slowly roll the nori up.
Seal the moistened end.
Give a gentle squeeze to the mat with the roll inside.
Unroll the mat and cut the roll in half. Then cut each half in half again, and then into 1-inch rounds.
Eat plain or with a dipping sauce.

Building Blocks for Maki Rolls

- avocado
- blanched daikon

- blanched greens
- cooked tempeh or tofu
- cucumbers
- nut butter
- pickles or sauerkraut
- sprouts

The Need for Weed (Seaweed with Rice)

- 1 cup organic short grain brown rice, soaked in 2 cups water 6 hours or overnight
- 1-inch piece of kombu soaked in water until soft (discard water)
- 1/3 cup dried arame
- 1 teaspoon toasted sesame oil
- 1 carrot, minced
- 1/2 sweet onion, diced
- 1/2 cup apple juice or water
- 1 tablespoon shoyu
- 1 tablespoon minced parsley or cilantro

Place rice, soaking water, and kombu in a pot with lid on and bring to a boil.

Place flame deflector under pot and turn down heat to simmer. Simmer for 50 minutes.

Meanwhile, soak arame with enough water to cover for 20 minutes.

Discard water. Set aside.

Oil-sauté onion and carrot in skillet until soft.

Add arame to skillet.

Deglaze the pan with apple juice.

Simmer uncovered until all liquid is gone.

Add shoyu and simmer 3 more minutes to incorporate flavor.

Add rice to skillet and warm through.

Serve with fresh garnish.

Mermaid Salad

- 2-ounce package of arame
- 3–4 cups of cucumbers, thinly sliced. Use one variety or a combination of pickling, baby, and/or English cucumbers. To embellish the cucumber, drag a fork along the sides with moderate pressure to create decorative grooves.
- 1 large or 2 small tangerines, cut into small pieces
- 2 teaspoons shoyu
- 1/4 cup brown rice vinegar
- juice of 1/2 lemon
- 1 tablespoon toasted sesame oil
- 1/4 cup pan toasted sesame seeds

Rinse arame and soak for 30 minutes. Discard soaking water.

Place arame in a pan with 1/2 cup water on medium heat without a lid.

Cook until water has been evaporated.

Set aside to cool.

In a bowl, add cucumbers, tangerines, and arame.

Mix shoyu, vinegar, lemon, and oil to make a simple dressing.

Add dressing to arame salad and mix to combine.

Top with sesame seeds.

Substitute pomegranate seeds for tangerines for a holiday salad.

Serve the salad on a bed of fresh greens.

Serve the salad in individual lettuce cups.

Halt the Salt

Keeping a strong blood quality requires good quality minerals. The most common mineral we take in is salt. Salt makes the stomach's hydrochloric acid necessary for proper digestion, and digestion is the key to health and happiness. All salt is not created equal. If the salt you use comes in a cardboard container with a pour spout, it is refined salt and harsh on health, leading to high blood pressure. Some brands of salt are also highly processed with many additives, such as bleach, anti-caking chemicals, and high-fructose corn syrup. Processed foods, meaning any natural food that has been altered, packaged, and no longer contains its life force includes large amounts of refined salt. Refined salt is not a natural salt, and the body can't use it properly for natural functions.

Iodine in salt is not needed when living along the seacoast. The sea air provides enough iodine for proper thyroid function. Iodized salt can cause the same symptoms of iodine deficiency, such as goiter or thyroid cancer.

Salt made naturally through salt water evaporation is best. Salt should contain many minerals besides sodium and chloride. The amounts of minerals should be listed on the brand's website. I find gray and Himalayan salts too contractive since they are high in magnesium, but that is just my opinion. You may find them to be perfect for you. I recommend Eden Portuguese sea salt, Bonin, or SI salt. If you find these natural salts to be bland, it means you have become accustomed to high amounts of sodium and chloride in the brand of salt you use.

Salt is best for health when incorporated into cooked dishes. When salting water to cook pasta, the water should taste like the ocean. Go ahead and taste it. Adding salt at the table does not allow the integration of minerals into the food through the transformation of heat. Cooking with salt has a strengthening effect on health but adding salt at the table has a harsh contractive effect on the body and sets up sweet cravings.

Shoyu is a fermented food that offers good minerals, living enzymes, organisms, and protein with a salty taste. It is a combination of soybeans and wheat that is fermented for months. It is used in much of macrobiotic cooking. Shoyu is best when unpasteurized and without chemicals, additives, or sugar. My favorite is Nama Shoyu or Mitoku. Shoyu attracts acidity out of the blood. It contains the perfect balance of amino acids to balance grain.

When understanding the 1:7 ratio as mentioned earlier, we see that minerals are the governing factor for all whole food choices. This golden ratio found throughout nature implies that we follow this ratio in our dietary choices. The sequence of nutrients flows from a dense vibration to a lighter vibration. Minerals such as calcium and magnesium are examples of condensed energy. Our higher vibrations are nutrients such as love and faith.

Mineral/Protein/Carbohydrate/Water/Oxygen/Vibration/ Higher Vibration

- We need seven times more proteins than minerals.
- We need seven times more carbohydrates than proteins.
- We need seven times more water than carbohydrates.
- We need seven times more oxygen than water.
- We need seven times more vibration as the pulsation of life force, love, or connection to our source.
- We need seven times higher vibration than vibrations. These are subtle short waves and refined sublime vibrations that connect us directly to the infinite. We may not see them, but many people perceive them.

The mineral is the foundation of life. A strong stomach acid is required to absorb minerals. If there is one food available to all that contains this 1:7 ratio of nutrients, you will find it growing in a sunny field. Animal-based foods do not follow this natural proportion of nutrients. I bet you can guess what does.

Chapter 13

Sweet Treats

Sweetness is important in a balanced life when eating grain and veggies. This is especially true for children. I recommend enjoying dessert two or three times per week and on special occasions (real special occasions—not Black Friday!).

Bars for the Stars

- 1 cup raw, unsalted organic sunflower seeds
- 1 cup raw, unsalted organic pumpkin seeds
- 1 cup sesame seeds
- 1/2 cup pine or favorite nut
- 1/2 cup organic brown rice syrup

Rinse the seeds and nuts in a strainer with water and toss into a hot cast-iron skillet.

With a wooden utensil, keep them moving to prevent burning. They will release their fragrance and begin to pop when fully toasted. Meanwhile, add syrup into a small pot and heat to a simmer.

Pour hot syrup into seed mixture and stir to combine.

As it cools, you can mix with your hands.

Spread on a cutting board and let fully cool.

Cut into shapes or roll into balls and serve.

You may put them in individual mini muffin papers for a pretty arrangement.

Add-ins include raisins, chopped, dried apricots, dried cherries, currants, nondairy chocolate bits, or any dried confection that you like.

Bars for the Stars

Happy Day Parfait

- 2 cups organic apple juice or white grape juice. I really like Martinelli's apple juice. It costs more, but the flavor is superior, and it comes in a glass bottle.
- pinch of salt
- 3 tablespoons agar flakes
- 1/2–1 cup brown rice syrup, flavored brown rice syrup, or maple syrup, according to taste
- 2 heaping tablespoons kudzu diluted in 1/4 cup of cold water
- 2 teaspoons organic lemon zest
- 2 cups fruit, fresh or frozen (strawberries, blueberries, raspberries, peaches, cherries, or apricots)

In a pot, combine apple juice, salt, agar, and sweetener.

Bring to a boil and lower heat to a simmer.

Simmer until agar flakes are dissolved, approximately 5–10 minutes. Whisk in diluted kudzu. To avoid clumping, begin to whisk before adding kudzu and add the kudzu slowly while whisking.

Continue stirring for 3–5 minutes until juice mixture becomes translucent. Remove from heat.

Stir in lemon zest and fruit.

Mash by hand or puree in a blender.

Pour into serving bowl, individual cups, pie plate, or layer in a parfait glass.

Top with cashew cream (page 232) or almond cream. (page 233)

Change the juice and fruit according to the season.

Individual Happy Day Parfait with Cashew Creme

Happy Day Parfait in Pie Form

> 🌾 Kudzu or kuzu is a starch from the kuzu plant that is used as a macrobiotic medicinal ingredient as well as a culinary thickener. Kuzu is a climbing vine that reaches heights of a full foot. While it grows wildly in the South, it is seen as a nuisance.

Kuzu has proven itself to be highly effective in soothing the gastrointestinal tract. The beta-glucan contained in this powder provides a powerful anti-inflammatory quality, and it is instrumental in the natural treatment of Crohn's, colitis, reflux, and many other gastrointestinal disorders. Kuzu is high in genistein and daidzein, two isoflavones that have strong anti-tumor effects. Even a hangover can be treated with kuzu.

The flavonoid composition of Pueraria, which is found in kudzu, counteracts free radicals. Many have included kuzu in their treatment of gastrointestinal disorders, headaches, influenza, fever, anxiety, hypertension, migraines, muscular tension, and allergies. Because kuzu heals the gut—where all health begins—it is valuable for most health conditions. Kuzu also lowers blood sugar. The phytoestrogens in kuzu has proven helpful with menopausal hot flashes. The common cold does not stand a chance when kuzu is on board.

Hot-off-the-press research is showing its usefulness in alcohol withdrawal and recovery. The isoflavone daidzein found in kuzu interferes with the metabolism of alcohol. It produces effects similar to the drug Antabuse, which is currently used in the treatment of alcoholism. That's some root! As kuzu grows, it amazingly nourishes the soil.

Purchase kuzu in its dry, chunky form. Dilute kuzu in a bit of cold water. Hot water will cause clumping. Use one tablespoon of kuzu per cup of liquid for a thickener. Kuzu offers your dish a glistening appearance. To avoid clumping when adding to a dish, begin whisking before adding kuzu and continue whisking until fully incorporated.

Kayla Loves Cashew Cream

- 2 cups raw and unsalted cashews, soaked in 1 1/2 cups water overnight
- 1/4 cup brown rice or maple syrup to taste
- pinch of salt
- 1 teaspoon organic vanilla extract

Place cashews and soaking water in a pot with a lid and cook on low until soft, approximately 15 minutes.

Place cooled cashews with water, sweetener, salt, and vanilla in a blender and turn on high until thick and creamy.

Add water for desired consistency.

I have found my daughter-in-law eating cashew cream by the spoonful right out of my fridge, hence the name.

Add apple juice to thin consistency as an option.

The addition of a tablespoon of tahini or almond butter turns cashew cream into a rich pudding.

Cashew Crème over Peach Happy Day Parfait

Almond Cream

- 1 cup organic almonds soaked in 2 cups water overnight
- 1/2 cup water
- 1/2 cup organic brown rice syrup
- 1/2 teaspoon lemon juice
- 1/4 teaspoon sweet white miso
- 1 tablespoon organic vanilla extract
- 1/4 teaspoon organic almond extract

Squeeze the soaked almond with your fingers, and the skin will pop off.

Simmer the peeled almonds on low heat for 10 minutes in a pot with a lid. Add water if necessary.

When cooled, blend almonds in a blender until it becomes a fine meal.

Add the 1/2 cup of water, syrup, lemon, and miso and continue to blend.

Add vanilla and almond extracts and blend until smooth.

Use as a dessert nondairy topping.

Chestnut Puree

- 1 cup dried chestnuts
- 2 cups water
- organic brown rice syrup to taste

Soak chestnuts overnight in water and then pressure-cook in same water on full pressure for 45 minutes.

Place chestnuts and water in blender.

Add enough syrup to desired sweetness.

Blend until smooth and creamy.

Use as a dessert nondairy topping.

No-Hoof Gelatin

Kanten is a gelatin dessert known in macrobiotics. A sweet kanten can be made from any dried or fresh fruit or juice. A kanten can be savory as an aspic by thinly slicing vegetables and cooking them with herbs and vegetable broth. Agar (a type of sea vegetable) is used as the gelling agent.

Lemon Kanten

- 2 cups organic apple or white grape juice diluted with 1 cup water
- 4 tablespoons agar flakes
- pinch of salt
- 2 tablespoons maple syrup
- 1/2 cup organic brown rice syrup
- 1/2 teaspoon vanilla or lemon extract
- Optional: 1/2 teaspoon cardamom or a pinch of fresh or powdered ginger
- 1/3 cup freshly squeezed lemon juice
- zest of 1 lemon

Place first 3 ingredients in a pot and bring to a boil.

Turn the heat to low and simmer until agar is completely dissolved (approximately 5–10 minutes).

Add the next 3 ingredients and optional spice.

Continue to simmer another minute.

Turn the heat off and add the lemon juice and zest. Stir to combine. Serve in a large bowl or individual cups.

To make a different-flavored kanten, switch out the lemon and zest for 1 cup fresh or frozen fruit.

Top with a nut cream and mint leaf and a decorative slice of lemon on the rim of the dish.

Fruit Crumble

Topping

- 1 1/2 cup muesli mix (I like Bob's Red Mills) or plain oatmeal
- 1/2 cup whole wheat pastry flour
- 1/2 cup walnuts, chopped
- pinch of salt
- 1/4 cup extra-virgin olive oil
- 4 tablespoons maple syrup
- 1 teaspoon cinnamon

Preheat oven to 350 degrees.

Mix all ingredients in a large mixing bowl and set aside.

In a separate bowl, mix:

3/4 cup organic apple juice

1 heaping tablespoon diluted kudzu in 2 tablespoons cold water

pinch of salt

1 teaspoon organic vanilla extract

Set aside.

Place 3 cups of sliced fruit in a 9 x 12 baking dish.

Choose fruit according to the season. Cold season: 2 apples and 1 pear. Green or Cortland apples are ideal. Warm season: Berries, sliced peaches, plums, or a combination of fruits.

Pour the juice mixture over the fruit.

Crumble the dry mixture on top of the fruit.

Bake uncovered 45 minutes or until fruit juices are bubbly.

Serve warm and top with a nondairy dessert topping.

Snap, Crackle, and Crunch Treats

- 1 cup organic brown rice syrup
- 1/2 cup almond or peanut butter
- 1 teaspoon sweet white miso
- 3 cups puffed brown rice cereal

Mix syrup and butter and heat over low flame.

Dilute miso in 1/2 teaspoon water and add to pot.

Turn off heat.

Place cereal in a bowl and pour hot mixture over it.

Mix well.

Spread over a cutting board and cut into shapes or roll into balls.

You may add dried fruit or nuts as an option.

Rice by the Pound

- 2 cups organic sweet brown rice
- 2 cups water
- pinch of salt
- 1/2 cup toasted sesame seeds

Soak rice in 2 cups water overnight.

Place rice, soaking water, and salt in a pressure cooker and bring up to pressure.

Place a flame tamer under the pot and turn heat to low, maintaining pressure.

Cook for 45–50 minutes.

Bring down pressure naturally.

Place in a wooden bowl.

Pound the rice with a pestle or surikogi until about 50 percent of the rice is broken down. You'll notice it getting sticky.

Sing your favorite song or think happy thoughts as you pound. The strength of pounding and good vibes energizes and strengthens the rice.

Form the rice dough into small balls and roll in sesame seeds.

Options for other tasty toppings: a thin coating of brown rice syrup and rolled-in toasted nuts, pureed chestnuts, or fruit preserves.

Apply thin coat of almond cream (page 233) and roll in toasted nuts or toasted sesame seeds.

A Is for Apple

- 4 large apples (Cortland, Granny Smith, or Rome)
- 2 tablespoons sunflower seeds
- 1 tablespoon walnuts
- 1/2 teaspoon cinnamon
- 2 teaspoons barley miso
- 8 tablespoons tahini

Preheat oven to 375 degrees.

Slice off the top of each apple to act as a lid.

Core the apples with a corer or knife, making a 1-inch opening.

Toast the seeds and nuts by rinsing them in a strainer and adding them into a hot cast-iron pan or skillet.

Toss the seeds and nuts around in the skillet until fragrant and fully toasted.

Mix the seeds and nuts with the remaining ingredients.

Fill the center of the apples with the stuffing.

Top with the cover.

Bake for 45 minutes or until apples are soft.

You may also add raisins or other minced dried fruit.

Hot Molo

- 1 1/2 tablespoons barley malt
- 3/4 cup water
- 1 cup almond milk

Heat water and milk in a small saucepan.

Stir in malt and heat through.

Pour into mug or thermos.

This recipe originally was made with molasses, which explains the name. I changed the molasses to barley malt to avoid simple sugars, and the flavor is even better. Barley malt tastes amazingly like molasses. Now I may call it Out of the Vault Malt.

There's a Bean in My Truffle

- 1 cup azuki beans soaked in 3 cups water for 6 hours or overnight
- 1-inch piece of kombu soaked in water until soft (discard water)
- 1 cup raisins or minced Medjool dates
- 2 tablespoons maple syrup to taste

Toppings

Place the beans, water, kombu, and raisins in a pressure cooker.

Seal the lid and bring up to high pressure.

Place a flame deflector under pot.

Lower heat to maintain pressure and cook for 30 minutes.

Bring pressure down naturally.

Remove lid and stir in maple syrup.

Let mixture cool.

Form into truffle-sized balls.

Roll into chopped nuts, dried coconut, jam, cocoa powder, or kinako powder.

> Kinako powder is made from ground roasted soybeans and can be purchased on Amazon.
> This recipe can also be spread into a baking dish, sprinkled with toppings, and cut into squares.

There's a Bean in My Truffle

Satisfying desserts without sugar will reward our health, stabilize our moods, and trim our waistlines. Natural sweetness creates happiness in ways that sugar cannot. The reasons why sugar will not make for lasting happiness are many. Here are the top contenders:

- The sweetness of sugar may liven your taste buds and make you feel good in the moment. Each time we eat sugar, it is quickly absorbed into our blood, it peaks, and like a quick blast of combustion, we crash—each and every time up to several times a day! But like sex without love, the feeling is short-lived and superficial. Or like chewing gum, the flavor is brief—and you're left chewing polyisobutylene!

- Sugar is highly refined from what was a whole food grown in tropical climates. The vitamins, minerals, molasses, enzymes, and fiber are stripped away. Chemicals such as sulfur dioxide, lye, phosphoric acid, calcium hydroxide, and polyacrylamides are used in the processing of making sugar. Think of it as an addictive chemical bath. Some sugar is bleached with bone char made from animals, and not all sugar is vegan.
- Sugar weakens the villi (absorbing fingerlike projections that line the small intestine) and strongly affects the biome. Where does all health begin? That's right. In the gut.
- Sugar has been replaced in most sweet foods by high-fructose corn syrup. It is cheap and sweet, and we love it. Fructose is more expansive to energy than sugar and can create stagnation of energy flow. High-fructose corn syrup is expansive enough to blow out the entire chakra and auric systems, and it is pretty much in everything we eat. Fructose converts directly into body fat. It is metabolized by the liver and is not able to be stored like sugar. This is not good news for our figures. The energy of sugar and fructose rises sharply to the higher chakras, leaving you with a feeling of brain fog, ungrounded, and scattered thinking. Intuition and direction in life are lost. The iron that is part of a red blood cell is magnetic. When blood quality weakens from sugars, and the blood is anemic, the transmission of universal energy and our higher self is staticky. We become lost in our own lives.
- Inflammation is the outcome of extreme expansion from sugar. Just as a garden hose provides the structure for water to flow, narrowing the diameter extensively or expanding the structure extensively will impede and eventually stop the stream of water. This is exactly how life force flows through our bodies. Sugar is the extensive expansion that will impede our energy. Nothing good ever grows from stagnation. Because we are holistic beings, every aspect of us becomes expanded: heart (congested heart failure), kidneys (glomerular nephritis), colon (constipation), and emotions (fear, anxiety, and paranoia). This accounts for any and all expansion in the body. Conditions that we would

think are not related to diet actually are because all foods carry an energetic vibration. We would not consider conditions such as a herniated disk, hemorrhoids, or plantar fasciitis as a food-related condition, but a diet change will correct the expanded tissue and extinguish the fire of inflammation. You will know the kids are too expanded by their night terrors or incessant whining!
- Sugar can lower our vibration to that of bacteria and viruses. We attract what we resonate with. The best assurance to prevent viral infections is a strong blood quality and immune system.

In New England, autumn arrives with chilly temperatures. Vitamin D levels begin to drop as less time is spent outside in the sunshine. High sugar holidays follow—Halloween, Thanksgiving, Christmas, and Valentine's Day—and this combination is an invitation to influenza. Best to keep your vitamin D levels at 80ng/ml and skip the sugar feast.

The quality of the blood is the foundation for health. The red blood cells that are produced in our bodies today are made from the foods we ate yesterday. A red blood cell lives for 120 days. This means that it takes four months to completely change the quality of our blood from animal to plant. The most important way to maintain blood quality is through balanced plant eating. Sugar is a plant that is tropical in nature and highly refined, and it weakens the blood. I would like to repeat that 8,830,485 times! I think of it as the devil that leads us to temptation and strikes when we are weakened by its sweetness.

Our blood cells are produced directly from what is absorbed in our small intestines. The vibration it carries will determine your fate. The foods we eat create the blood that reaches every cell in our bodies. If blood quality is too hot (yang) from contractive foods such as animal protein, hard-baked flour, or poor-quality salt, an imbalance occurs as well as sweet cravings.

The same is true when the blood quality is too cold (yin) from over-expansive foods from sugar, dairy, alcohol, coffee, and chocolate (most food from the tropics) and creates a craving for hard, crunchy, salty, cured, and animal-based foods. The imbalance prevents the connection to nature that makes us happy. The imbalance determines our temperament, thoughts, and choices.

For instance, when wearing yang glasses, everyone around you seems weak, inefficient, or incompetent, especially when driving. We blame others when our energy is too tight. The mind will not open to see another view or opinion, and stubbornness rules your life. When our mind cannot open, our experiences become limited. When wearing yin glasses, everyone around you seems pushy, rude, and aggressive. We create our condition every day by the foods we eat, which become our blood quality. Happiness occurs when eating foods that are balanced in the middle of the yin and yang scale, such as grain, beans, and vegetables. Vegetable vibration is higher than animal or man-made vibration. It can be felt in our bodies if we pay attention to it. Food makes the blood, blood makes the cells, cells make the tissue, tissue makes the organs, organs make the system, and the system makes you! The vibration woven throughout the blood and the organs is our consciousness. Is yours on a high playing field or is it like an animal?

If a tree has a disease, one can pick off the diseased leaves to remedy the problem, but that will not change the health condition of the tree. Until the soil is treated, the tree will slowly perish. Metaphorically, sugar weakens the soil. No happiness there. The blood is equivalent to the soil, and the organs are equivalent to the leaves. Organs can be removed, but if the underlying blood condition is not addressed, suffering is inevitable. When we recognize our participation in sickness, the cure is evident—and we can work on the underlying cause. We are responsible for the contribution to our health and happiness or our pain and despair.

Sugar is a simple carbohydrate that will spike your insulin level and create the need for more sugar. Its addictive nature keeps us coming back for more, which is why it is in all processed foods. Do not be a slave to sugar. When we are addicted, we lose our freedom. The freedom of our lives comes with a huge price tag:

- happiness
- freedom to live openly
- freedom to choose what food to eat
- freedom from cravings
- freedom from medical appointments
- freedom from physical pain and stiffness

- freedom from internal stress
- free to watch our loved ones thrive
- free to be happy
- free to act like rice

Sugar creates acidic blood that leaches the alkaline minerals from the body, such as calcium, B vitamins, phosphorous, and iron, which can manifest as osteoporosis, anemia, anxiety, depression, and other conditions. The feeling of a hangover is the result of depleting all the water-soluble vitamin B through excessive urination. That is what vitamin and mineral depletion feels like. Your daily exhausted feeling, attitude, and defeated outlook may be a symptom of the sugar-depleting effect of your cannoli.

Bacteria, viruses, and cancers thrive in an acidic sweet environment. We know this because to culture a bodily fluid to check for infection, a sample is spread on a petri dish to identify which bacteria is growing. The culture medium in the petri dish is made of a sugared material called nutrient agar. Bacteria, viruses, and cancers thrive in sweet blood.

The only food source for viruses is sugar. Therefore, when we fall ill to influenza or other viruses, we lose our appetites. Nature finds a way to starve the virus to death. Aren't we amazing?

I taught my children that sugar harms the Pac-Men that eat up the bad germs in our bodies. Understand that white blood cells are disabled by 40 percent for up to five hours after consuming an average soda. It's a visual they will always remember.

Sugar feeds the bad gut bacteria and harms the healthy ones. This alone can be detrimental to our physical and mental well-being.

Bacteria in the mouth digest the sugar debris on the teeth and causes decay. It not only causes tooth decay, it causes you decay. Sugar does not just weaken your teeth—it weakens you! Energetic stagnation breeds disease and decay of all human tissue. Gross!

Sugar and corresponding insulin levels create hills and valleys of emotion throughout the day. The same stressor triggers a different reaction in us, depending on our blood glucose level at the time. When we stop eating refined sugar, we reestablish emotional stability and become more rational.

Sugar is dehydrating. Lifeless dehydrated skin makes us look older than we are.

Sugar is great for making mucus. Nasal congestion, sputum, cough, vaginal discharge, and other slippery effects of mucus are defined by the amount of sugar in the blood. When we have taken in too much sweetness from soda, candy, and other sugary treats, our amazing bodies will discharge the excess through the organs of elimination. Lungs discharge mucus as snot, sore throats, and coughs. The skin—our largest organ of elimination—discharges sugar in many ways from freckles to skin cancer. The colon will discharge via diarrhea. This happens most when summer turns to fall. The temperature increases atmospheric pressure and squeezes excessive expansive energy outward to maintain homeostasis. The symptoms of a cold are a direct reflection of what you have eaten during the prior season.

Sugar lacks fiber. Fiber feeds the biome. It is a lot of calories for no gut benefit.

Once sugar is detoxed from your blood, you will no longer crave that doughnut. In fact, you may find the taste of it repulsive!

The recommended dietary allowance (RDA) of refined white sugar is zero.

A small amount of a natural sweetener a few times a week will keep us in the happy zone. Maple syrup is a simple sugar, and though it is a natural source, it will affect insulin levels. Use sparingly. Its energy is more appropriate than tropical sugars if living in a four-season climate, and it can be used sparingly in a food-happy diet.

Artificial sweeteners have an even greater expansive effect on the body and should be avoided at all costs. They can also lower serotonin levels and disturb sleep.

Those on low-carb diets should beware of the coconut, monk fruit, jackfruit sugars, stevia, and sugar alcohols. They may be glycemic index-approved, but the accumulative effects can contribute to depression or anxiety when taken in excess. They are sweeter and more expansive than sugar and are not all gut friendly. In my practice, I have seen mood improve when sweeteners are removed from the diet.

To satisfy the sweetness we deserve, try a complex carbohydrate derived from grain, such as brown rice syrup or barley malt, in small amounts. Although less expansive, a grain-based sweetener should still be used modestly.

Chapter 14

Life without Breath

Breath equates life. We take our first breath at birth and our last breath at death. We take millions of breaths in between these times. We breathe every minute of every day, yet it is something we take for granted. The way we breathe reflects the way we live. We have unconscious breathing patterns just as we have energy patterns. By observing our natural breath, we learn to flow with the river rather than swim. The volume we take in with each breath shows our relationship to life and how much self-worth we carry.

Full breath equals strong self. Shallow breath equals weak self.

Notice a few ways that our breathing reflects our living. When we are shocked, we take in a sharp deep breath and hold it for a split second as we stop living. Try it. Pretend to hear shocking news.

Some of us exhale with a slight sound of effort at the end of exhalation, showing the hard challenge of life. This is noticeable when caring for people in pain.

A deep sigh with a long exhalation shows our defeat in a situation. It tells us that we have conceded.

Since the mind and body influence our breath, we can influence our minds and bodies through the conscious control of breathing. There are many benefits to conscious breathing. It increases oxygen in the body, relieves muscular tension, detoxifies skin, and integrates repressed aspects of ourselves. The breath allows a safe way to release the effects of trauma and witness the transformation from pain to joy.

Working with the breath will also melt the emotional and physical armor that protects us from past experiences. It provides clarity of thought and connects us to spirit. It is difficult to monitor our own breathing because our patterns feel natural to us. Have someone monitor your breathing pattern while at rest, during activity, and at times of stress—and begin noticing the breathing patterns of others. Knowing how we take in life through breath shows us where life force is blocked. We can manipulate our breath to enhance our lives. Set aside ten or fifteen minutes daily without distraction and practice these breathing exercises to find the one that suits you best. Explore a new one each day. Set a timer to avoid being aware of the time:

- Breathe in and out of nose. Sitting in a comfortable position with a straight spine, take in a deep breath and release it. Simply sit still and breathe naturally in through your nose and out through your nose. Without any judgment, make a mental note of how it feels in your nose, your chest, and your mind.
- In nose and out mouth. While sitting in a comfortable position, close your eyes, take in a big breath, and release it. Now is the time set aside for you and only you. Begin breathing in through your nose and out through your mouth. Notice if you feel tension anywhere in your body.
- In mouth and out nose. Sitting in a comfortable position, breathe in through your mouth and out through your nose. At the end of fifteen minutes, notice any changes made to your physical body or your thoughts.
- In mouth and out mouth. Sitting in a comfortable position, take in a big breath and let it go. Begin breathing in through your mouth and out through your mouth. How does it feel? Any difference from other styles of breathing?
- Counting breath. This breathing exercise can be done while sitting, lying down, or walking. With focus on the breath, take in a big breath and exhale. As you begin to breathe, count in breath one, out breath two, in breath one, out breath two. This breathing pattern can really relieve stress and tension.

- Block left nostril, breathe in right. Block right nostril, exhale left. Holding your thumb against your right nostril and your index finger against your left nostril, apply pressure to your index finger and breathe in through your right nostril. To exhale, release the index finger and apply pressure to your thumb and exhale through your left nostril. Repeat. Continue this breathing style for the designated time. Notice how each breath reveals a part of you to explore. Allow energy to move within you without controlling it.
- Block right nostril, breathe in left. Block left nostril, exhale right. Find a comfortable position. Take in a deep breath and release. Holding your thumb against your right nostril and your index finger against your left nostril, apply pressure to your thumb and breathe in through your left nostril. To exhale, release the thumb, apply pressure to your index finger, and exhale through your right nostril. Repeat. Continue this breathing pattern for the allotted time. Once you've established a rhythm, bring your focus to any part of your body that needs attention and bring the breath into that part with your awareness.
- Alternate 6 and 7. Assume a comfortable position. Take a deep breath and let it go. Use the same hand position as above. Block the left nostril and breathe in the right nostril; release the left nostril and apply pressure to the thumb and exhale out the left nostril. Keep the thumb blocking right nostril and breathe in the left nostril. Release the thumb, block the left nostril, and exhale through the right nostril. Repeat. Continue this breathing technique until time is up.
- Single nostril breathing. Sit in a relaxed way and take in a deep breath and exhale. Feeling sluggish? Try breathing in and out from the right nostril only. This will activate rising energy in your body and balance the chakras. Feeling scattered? Breathe in and out the left nostril only to bring balance to the center and calm energy.
- The fully connected breath. This breathing exercise is immensely powerful and is the reward for mastering the ones before it. Also called *circular breathing*, the inhale and the exhale are connected

as one to increase the life force. You will experience the opening of your chakras where the deepest self is visible to you. This is a very vulnerable place for most of us. We can quickly peek inside or stay there a while. It is an opportunity to release what blocks us from moving forward and claim our inner power. We can only do this by going deep within and beyond the ego and mind. This breath will open the muscles in the belly that we unconsciously close off. We naturally belly breathe as babies up to age twelve. Then we learn how to manage stress by holding our breath. The fully connected breath allows us to reach an alpha state in consciousness, where we release negative self-talk and learn to fully listen to the self. We can reprogram our beliefs and thoughts. This is where the deepest healing occurs. Exploring the inner landscape and surrendering to change is what it's all about. We melt the gaps between the separated parts of ourselves and become whole.

Aristotle once said, "The soul never thinks without a picture." The unconscious mind works with pictures, images, and dreams. When we touch our inner souls, we communicate this way without words. We find our answers and solutions when we allow our pain to transform into joy from this place, and it will. Healing is like peeling an onion; each layer may bring a tear until we reach the center of sweetness.

This practice may take up to an hour and is best if shared with a trusted loved one. One partner will read the exercise aloud while the other partner breathes. This allows you to learn and perfect this breathing technique. It may take several attempts over time to master, and it may test your patience. Another option is to make a recording of the instructions and play it for yourself. It may be tedious to learn, but in the end, you may find incredible transformation and peace—maybe even enough to write a book of your own!

Music and sound play a major role in this experience. To enhance the session, play background music that assists the spirit in moving inward. Stimulating music and drumming, tribal music, or any activating music that blocks out the world for you will help guide you to the alpha state. Here are a few of my choices: *To Russia with Love* by Chip Davis, *Harts,*

Hands, and Hides: A Shamanic Journey into Native Drumming of the Americas by Talking Taco Music Inc., and *The Soundtrack to Rocky* by Bill Conti. Breathing to the same music every day creates a cellular memory in the body. Over time, your body will hear the music and automatically assist you in achieving an alpha state because our chakras and breathing are deeply intertwined with our central nervous systems.

To breathe deeply, an unrestricted waistband will be necessary. Are you ready to go beyond the mind to where truth resides and meet the real you?

Turn off your phone and set aside this time for you. Create a safe and comfy space. Have a blanket nearby in case you get chilly. Lie flat in a comfortable position and relax. Begin by taking in a deep breath and letting it go. Breathe normally and notice how your body feels and any thoughts you may have. Spend time naturally breathing to become inured with your breath. After several minutes, notice how there is a natural pause between the end of exhalation and the beginning of inhalation. Bring your focus into the breath and breathe in rhythm with the music. Be sure not to hyperventilate. For a few moments, you may allow your mind to be active while your energies settle in. Now begin to bring your awareness inward. Bring your attention to your feet. Scrunch them up and tighten them for five seconds and release. Take a deep breath in and out. Tighten the muscles of your thighs and hold it for five seconds and release. Take a deep breath and let it go. Tighten the muscles of your buttocks and hold it for five seconds and relax. Take in another deep breath and sigh. Tighten your abdominal muscles and hold it tightly for five seconds and rest. Take another deep breath and exhale. Tighten your shoulder and chest muscles for five seconds and let go. Take another deep breath. Notice any thoughts or feelings that occur during this time. Just notice. Do not try to change anything that you feel. Now scrunch up your facial muscles and hold them tightly for five seconds—and finish with a deep breath.

Push your belly out as far as it will extend. In this moment, be proud of your belly. No girdles or sucking it in. Let it be free and large. Breathe in as you push the belly out. Bring the breath past the diaphragm and into your belly. Relax the belly upon exhalation. Practice this for several minutes. With each breath, the belly expands. Place your hands where the belly meets the pubic bone and bring the breath deep into that place. Push your hands off your pubic bone with your breath. Continue to breathe deeply into this place and feel your hands rise and fall with your breath. This opens the second chakra—the seat of the soul. With each breath, bring your awareness along with the breath into the deepest part of your belly. This is usually very tight, and it may take some effort. As the chakra opens, you may feel a fine tremor in the lower abdominal muscles. Yay! That's the place. It may be uncomfortable at first—enough that you might want to quit—but be gentle with yourself and continue the practice.

When you find this magic spot deep within the belly, you may begin deepening the practice. Begin by pushing your belly out and fill it with air and then fill the chest with air to capacity and let it go slowly and with control. Before the exhalation is complete, push the belly out again with an inhalation, starting a new cycle. When the belly is filled with air, fill the chest with air and then slowly exhale. Before exhalation is complete, push the belly out and bring the breath into the belly. Practice this until the coordination of belly and breathing is smooth. There is no separation or pause between exhalation and inhalation. That is it! The connected breath.

Continue this breath until you have reached a place of knowing or become fatigued. The average is forty-five minutes to an hour. Have your partner at your side to assist and support you. Do not hyperventilate. Breathe slowly and deliberately. When you feel ready to end the practice, rest and breathe normally. You may return to the connected breath after a few moments of rest if you wish. You will know when you have had enough. Simply rest and allow the energies to settle. Take as much time as you need. Change the music to soothe and support you. Anything by Steven Halperin will bring the spirit back home and allow you to integrate the new energy. You may feel emotions arise or an uncomfortable uneasiness in your body. It is not uncommon to see images or have memories. It is all part of the process. Notice any changes in yourself for the next few days. There is no limit to the extent of transformation in your life. You are on your way. Combine this with high-vibrational food, meridian tapping, chakra healing, and grain eating, and you will not even recognize yourself!

> In a normal waking state, we are in beta brain waves. These brain waves cycle thirteen times per second. We are focused on the outside world and our agendas. An alpha state is entered when brain waves slow down to eight to twelve cycles per second. This state of consciousness is the meditative mind, a tasmic state, (a deeply relaxed state while maintaining awareness) and the door to the subconscious. The theta state is four to seven cycles per second and is entered in deep rest and dreams. This is where transcendental meditation exists. The delta state is entered when brain waves cycle three times or less times per second. This state is deep sleep. Gamma waves are the newest to be discovered. They are important for learning and excitation. All states of mental integrity are affected by breathing. Breathing and meditation have been shown to be effective in the treatment of all levels of mental health, including ADHD, depression, anxiety, impulsivity, as well as whatever is considered "normal."

The physical act of breathing circulates the life-giving energy throughout the chakra and meridian system. Sedentary breathing slows energy flow. Intense breathing with extreme exercise can halt energy flow. Breathing while walking through nature activates the natural flow of universal energy in harmony with our energy. It is recharging.

Chapter 15

The Invisible Invaders

While eating grain, chewing, and breathing bring happiness, a dirty environment can take it away. There are many pollutants that we are exposed to every day. Some we can avoid, and others we cannot. Every toxin that you can eliminate from your blood is one more day of happiness for you.

Many may not take this seriously, but our blood contains hundreds of toxins that were not found in human blood in the 1950s. This is a serious situation. The toxic chemicals we use every day become commonplace to us, and we lose the importance of what we are in contact with. We, as consumers, need to be smart about what we consume. If we examine what we come into contact with every day, we will be able to choose what we are exposed to—right down to the bisphenol A that coats our cash register receipts. Our skin is the largest organ of the body and has great absorption ability. In medicine, pharmaceuticals are embedded in patches and applied to the skin for drug absorption. The administration of drugs via the skin is amazingly effective because the skin is highly absorptive to what is applied to it. We apply many products to our skin without much attention paid to the ingredients in our products.

Included in your high-priced moisturizer lurks a potential danger: parabens. A paraben is a preservative that retards bacterial growth and extends the shelf life of cosmetics, lotions, pharmaceuticals, and many foods. The seven parabens are: methylparaben, propylparaben, butylparaben, ethyl paraben, heptyl paraben, isobutyl paraben, and benzyl paraben. They have been used in combination with each other and with other preservatives since 1930. Butylparaben has been found to be the most dangerous to health. Effective against yeasts and molds, these additives can be found in an exceptionally long list of lotions, moisturizers, makeup, shampoos, sunscreens, deodorants, and most products that line the cosmetic aisle. Paraben is another name for hydroxybenzoic acid ester, and by law, it must be listed in the ingredients list. Parabens have an estrogenic effect and have been identified in breast tumors as concluded by Dr. Philippa Darbre. They are found inside of tumors (P.D.Darbre, 2004).

Parabens cross the placenta and can be found in breast milk. Our developing babies are infused with a toxic chemical cocktail from the products we use. The Environmental Working Group has found more than two hundred synthetic chemicals in baby's cord blood (Group, 2005).

Parabens are easily absorbed through the skin and accumulate in fatty tissue, particularly breast tissue. Read your labels. If an ingredient ends in the word paraben, put it back on the shelf.

It is no secret that plastic has become a problem in the world of pollution. Our oceans are in trouble because of the amount of plastics that are manufactured and consumed. What is not well-known is the amount of water pollution due to the fashion industry. Our clothing is made of synthetic materials that leach into the oceans from our washing machines. Our beloved yoga pants are a big offender. The buttery soft fabric is made from petroleum and microplastics that find their way into our oceans. Plastics and synthetics are found in the fish we eat. It is estimated that we consume a credit card-sized amount of plastic every day. We are becoming plasticized humans! Notice the toxic odor at a clothing store at the change of season when a new shipment of clothing arrives. It is the outgassing of chemicals from the materials. Choose natural fibers to be against your skin, such as bamboo or organic cotton (Press, 2017).

It is difficult to avoid the use of plastic. We live in houses surrounded with vinyl and petroleum-based and plastic furnishings and carpets. Plastic is being recycled into clothing and furniture. The newest outdoor decking is now made of plastic. Living among plastic creates a chaotic static electricity in our energy systems. Plastic breaks down as it ages, releasing its chemicals. For this reason, avoid reusing plastic water bottles. You may not know the amount of phthalate from plastic we consume every day. Phthalates are chemicals added to plastic to make it bendable, flexible, and durable. They are called plasticizers and have been proven to be another hormone disruptor, which acts like estrogen in the body. Food storage containers, water bottles, kitchen utensils, beauty products, nail polish, perfume, carpets, plastic wrap, toys, floor tiles, and enteric-coated medicine all contain this chemical. That new shower curtain smell is a hefty dose of phthalate. This plasticizer will not be seen on an ingredient list, but be assured if it plastic based and bendable, it contains phthalates. More than 90 percent of Americans have phthalates in their urine.

I have been speaking with several hospital suppliers to reduce the amount of phthalate exposure to patients through medical plastics such as IV fluid bags, IV tubing, and oxygen tubing. There are great products available for hospital use. Inquire at your local hospital what their practice is to reduce patient phthalate exposure.

When paper goods are bleached, a dioxin is created. Dioxins are a group of toxic chemicals considered carcinogenic by the World Health Organization. We find dioxins in many personal products that we use. Diapers, paper towels, napkins, and many animal products contain dioxins. My biggest concern is the use of tampons. Cotton and rayon are used to make tampons and they are genetically altered and sprayed with Roundup weed killer. Newer bleaching methods have reduced the amount of dioxin, but it remains present. These toxic vaginal sticks lie against the vaginal wall, creating inflammation of the vagina and cervix. Pay the extra cost for organic products. Some chemicals live with us forever. Want to check the safety of the products you and your family use? Ewg.org is a database of personal products and their tested safety reports.

All chemicals such as fungicides, pesticides, herbicides, and preservatives are stored in fat. The more fat you have, the more chemical load you carry. When we lose weight, the stored chemicals are released from the fat and reenter the bloodstream. Be prudent and purchase organic, natural products that bring you closer to an organic and natural life.

The MO on GMO

Genetically modified organisms entered our food supply in 1973. The cell structure of the plant is genetically altered to repel insects and increase crop yields. This is accomplished by forcing genes from one species into another. The desired DNA is implanted into the plant of a fruit, grain, or vegetable and grown in tissue culture. The new plant that grows will inherit the new DNA to resist pests. The crops are designed to resist the effects of glyphosate, the ingredient in Roundup weed killer. Glyphosate is then sprayed over the crop without consequence to the resistant crop.

Genetically altering the plant makes it sterile, and their seeds are appropriately called terminator seeds. This forces the farmer to purchase new seeds with each planting—from Monsanto, the maker of Roundup. Glyphosate chelates iron, manganese, zinc, and boron from the soil. Cross contamination of fields is common, and the GMO crop will infect the organic crop as its glyphosate-infused pollen spreads from one field to another. Monsanto then charges the organic farmer the cost of a GM product, and the contamination is such that organic farmland will never be rich and organic again (mathieuasselin, 2013) (FreelyGiveTruth2, 2013).

Plant genes are altered with glyphosate, which is present in the roots, stalks, leaves, and edibles. Corn, soy, cotton, and sugar beets are crops that are most heavily affected. Walk through a grocery store and try to find products that do not contain corn, corn oil, corn starch, corn syrup, wheat, flour, or soy and its by-products. We have a steady diet of glyphosate. If you purchase a food product that is not organic or labeled non-GMO, be certain that it contains glyphosate. To confuse the consumer further, GMO foods have been renamed biofortified. This toxic chemical accumulates in blood and tissue. Glyphosate has been found to be a hormone disrupter and causes genetic mutations. In recent news, glyphosate has been found responsible for causing cancer, specifically lymphoma. Glyphosate kills the bugs in the field and kills the bugs in our gut, weakening our biomes. Weak biomes equate to weak health and happiness.

The GMO crops are fed to the livestock that we eat. You will find its residue on the steak you prepare for dinner. Even the grass is GMO when you pay extra for grass-fed beef. Animals that have been fed GMO feed produce more inflammation in the body than naturally raised animals.

Soybeans used to make infant formula almost always come from a GMO crop.

There is a way to test urine for glyphosate:

https://www.greatplainslaboratory.com › glyphosate-test.

My last rant is about electricity.

When used properly, electricity is a safe and modern utility. It becomes dangerous if you stick your finger in a socket and get electrocuted. Eating electricity through food is also detrimental to health, but it is less dramatic. It drains the life force of the food it cooks. What happens to our food when we cook with electricity? Foods cooked in an electric skillet or crock pot have lost a portion of their life force. Plain and simple. Studies show that blood drawn at intervals after eating foods cooked with electricity reveals an increase in white blood cells. The body sees this food as foreign and sends white blood cells to get the invader. Electricity also damages the cell structure of vitamins. Notice how you feel after eating foods cooked with electricity and food cooked naturally. Foods cooked over a flame are energized with life force. Foods prepared by hand are infused with your strength and energy versus using a blender. If you must use an electric appliance for food preparation, allow the food to settle for a few minutes after its exposure. If you want to walk with a little snap in your step, throw away your microwave (mcw, 2002).

Because we are magnetic beings, electricity alters our chakras. Modern appliances in the home and office affect the natural flow of life force. Cancer rates are higher in families that live near high-tension wires because of this fact. Anything electric that touches you leaches your life force. Here's a few more examples: hair dryers, Instapots, blenders, electric mixers, computers, smartphones, heated car seats, electric blankets, electric cookware and ovens, earpods, and other technologies.

Smart appliances and smart meters have been creating health concerns. A smart appliance has a wave of wireless radiation from the appliance to your phone. This wave of radio frequency is running through your house—in your living space—as it communicates to the appliance. The more smart appliances in the home, the more exposure. Children are overly sensitive to wireless radiation because their bodies are small and more vulnerable. Their skulls are thin, making a device in their hands potentially hazardous. Children are now using devices at the age of two!

Wearing a smartwatch over your wrist meridians affects the flow of life force to the lungs, large intestine, heart, and digestion because those meridians are located at the wrist. Carrying your smartphone in a pocket can affect the body part that it rests against.

Bluetooth hearing aids and headphones are popular and communicate with each other by using a magnetic conduction field between the ears and through the skull and brain. Blue tooth is a type of EMF. Some people are sensitive to the radiation.

Maybe the idea of smart appliances is not so smart. To alleviate any concern, buy a smog meter and test the safety of your home. They cost about two hundred dollars—and are well worth it. You can also hire a professional for a total home assessment.

I recommend the Cornet ED-88TPlus EMF/RF Detector 100MHz–8GHz (Smart Meter Health Effects, 2020) (authors, 2017).

I also use a safe sleeve phone protector (safeSleeve, 2020).

(Irradiated A comprehensive compilation of the literature on radiofrequency fields and the negative biological impacts of non-iodizing electromagnetic fields on biological organisms, 2017)

We are now at the dawning of 5G or fifth-generation cellular wireless. It connects with other wireless networks and will enhance broadband dramatically. Because of its extreme electromagnetic range, every person, animal, and plant will not be able to escape the effects. It is interesting that the coronavirus outbreak was within a 5G hot spot. It is believed that the 5G exposure has a negative effect on the immune system, making people less resistant to viruses. Studies have not been done to confirm or deny this theory.

5G cellular wireless is a high-energy, millimeter-wave radiation source that affects our magnetic energy. It is predicted to have irreversible effects on health and the planet. It forms a grid of EMF pollution or dirty electricity in our homes and around our neighborhoods and cities. We live within that grid—and now we can download movies faster on our deathbeds. (Nine ways 5G and the internet of things will harm humans, wildlife, and earth, 2018).

While we are at it, we should have our homes and offices tested for radon. Radon is an invisible, odorless gas. Its tiny particles get trapped in lung tissue by breathing it in, and it is a major contributor to lung cancer.

It makes sense to choose all-natural products such as bedding, clothing, and furnishings to surround ourselves with natural fibers and vibrations. Plastic-coated cookware is no different. Teflon-coated pans when heated emit a gas, and when it is inhaled, it causes fluoropolymer fever, which is known as Teflon flu. Choose natural cookware such as cast-iron, stainless steel, and enamel-coated cast iron.

Bayer, the maker of Teflon, has paid out millions of dollars in lawsuits filed due to a variety of health concerns. Hundreds have come forward with documentation of cancer, ulcerative colitis, birth defects, and a host of other diseases that points to the use of the chemical used to make Teflon.

C-8, the chemical that makes nonstick happen, has been utilized in the manufacturing of water-repellant clothing and other fabrics, stain-resistant carpeting, food packaging, furniture, cosmetics, household cleaners, Scotchgard, waterproofing, self-cleaning ovens, pizza boxes, fast-food wrappers, and nail polish. Anything that resists grease and heat contains C-8. Love microwave popcorn? The lining of the bag contains C-8.

Studies show that perfluorooctanoic acid or C-8 has been found in the blood samples of 99 percent of humans *worldwide*. It has been found in drinking water throughout the world including remote, uninhabited places. It has been found in the water used to manufacture coffee, soda, and everything we eat. It has even been found in the bloodstream of the polar bear. Studies show that C-8 causes mice to overreact to allergens and may explain the rising cases of human allergies.

As consumers became aware of this toxic substance, Bayer decided to rename its poison GenX. C-8 cannot be broken down. It is here permanently. To minimize exposure to C8, do not use Teflon or any products that repel water, grease, or heat. We need to really think about our personal practices and choices. A high-grade water filter will eliminate drinkable C-8 and many other toxins.

Before you purchase a product, ask yourself three questions.

- Does it cause pollution and health risks in the manufacturing of this product?
- Does it cause pollution or health effects from the use of this product?
- Does it cause pollution or health effects to dispose of this product?

The earth pulsates with life and is self-cleaning and regenerating (like us). If the number of contaminants exceeds the earth's ability to adapt, future generations will be affected.

The Devil We Know: Netflix Documentary

Even in death, can we be happy and act like rice. A burial pod takes the place of a casket. It allows the safe decomposition of the remains in a pod. The pod is planted like a seed in a green cemetery with other pods. A tree is buried over the pod. You become the tree. The trees become a forest. One tree connects with the others and strengthens the whole. Let's act like rice. (Ecological burial pod turns bodies into trees, 2016)

The pod that contains the remains is constructed of biodegradable materials. It is buried in the ground, and a tree is planted over it. There is no wasted land like a cemetery. The forest will supply oxygen to the earth, and the visitors will enjoy the sounds of nature. I want mine to have a birdfeeder.

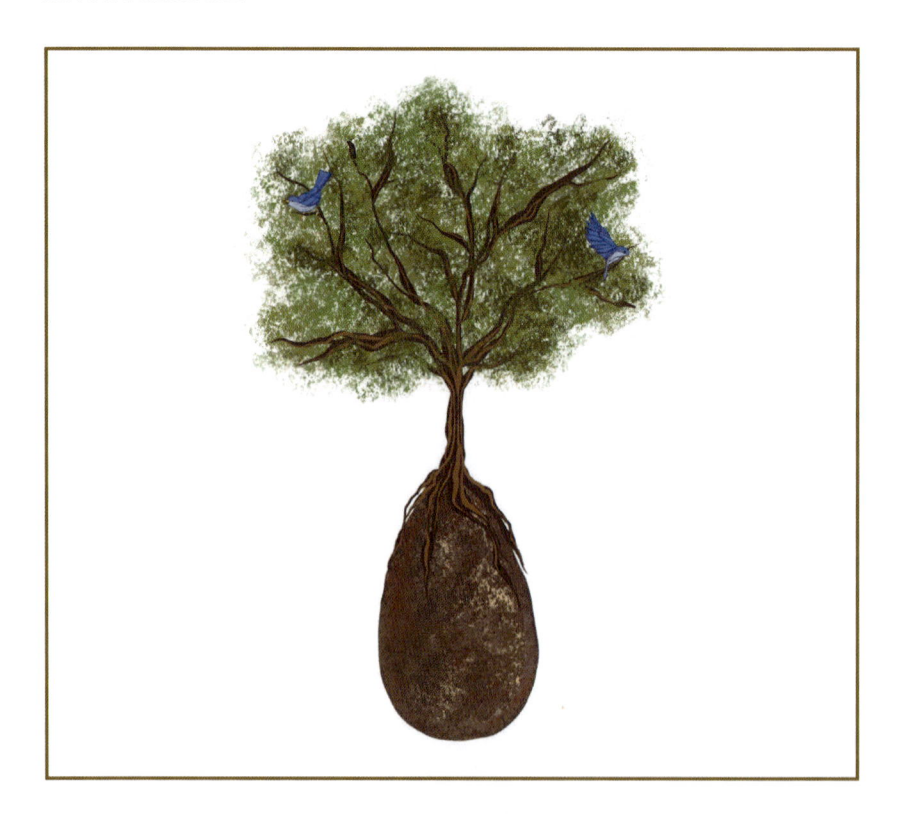

Chapter 16

You Will Know You're Acting Like Rice When ...

- You suddenly, for no reason, feel loved and cared for. This is especially noticeable if you live alone and have no family. This feeling can hit at any time so be prepared. It hit me while running to my next class at the Kushi Institute.
- You have a passion to share the love with others, especially those with opposing political or religious views. It is the understanding we seek without the threat. Love conquers the wanting to be right and removes the threat of other opinions.
- Feeling alive. Fatigue is a feeling of the past. We are digesting grain now. No more exhaustion from digesting heavy animals.
- You chew, breathe, align, and understand.
- Engaging in life. Noticing a healthy appetite for food, sex, exercise, knowledge, work, family, and anything else that lights your fire.
- Waking refreshed and restored. Deep sleep from eating grain is revealed when the energy body goes deep within itself and suspends. Ready to embrace the new day—whether it's hard physical labor, office life, or the stress of raising teenagers.
- You find your mind to be alert, sharp, and with great memory. We remember the feeling of universal oneness.
- You no longer need to be angry. When the internal organs are relaxed, we are relaxed. What once caused frustration and

impatience transcends into joy. Joyful living is a natural result of a natural life. Being angry shows us our limitations in thinking and reasoning. Being adaptive to cope with our ever-changing lives is limitless. Grain thinking gives us the capacity to accept our circumstances and change our misfortunes into opportunities. This is higher human thinking at its best!

- You glow! You may be stopped by strangers and asked what beauty moisturizer you use. Inner beauty radiates outward and is noticeably visible. Light bounces off your skin's reflection of a healthy blood quality. Your unpolished nails are healthy and resemble a French manicure. One day, I was asked to remove my clear nail polish at work, and I was not wearing any!
- The events in your life—both challenging and joyful—make perfect sense. Suffering ends. Everything we have encountered has shaped us into who we are today, and we are grateful.
- Appreciate all life. Never waste food, water, electricity, or other precious resources. We see value in all things, and gratitude is heightened. When significance is assigned to something, it becomes more important. Deep gratitude permeates our lives and gives meaning.
- The feeling of compassion is your driving force. Profits take a back seat to your heart's expression of love and oneness. You are a part of me, and I am a part of you. Love really does make the world go around.
- You want to share this knowledge with others. People will dismiss you with a condescending smile just as we did in the beginning of our transformation. It is okay. Everything happens at the right time. This is not theirs.
- You cannot contain all the happiness, and you explode—spilling joy everywhere.
- When those around you want to keep you down. Just as water seeks its own level, we resonate with the people around us who we connect with energetically. When we rise, it magnifies inefficiencies in others.
- You feel the oneness and become whole.
- You feel like a man in black.

At one time I did not know. I wrote this book for those who do not know. Now you know. We cannot unknow what we now know!

Chapter 17

It Took a Village

Rita Hefron

Rita was my massage instructor at the Polarity Realization Institute and a fellow registered nurse. Rita taught me to allow life energy to flow within me without controlling it. The first time I had to be the receiver of body work, I clenched my fists and endured the experience of being touched. She taught me to be as loved as the Velveteen Rabbit. Over time, I unclenched and embraced the notion of trust and the ability to receive. How beautiful. Thank you, Rita.

Nancy Risley

Nancy founded the Polarity Realization Institute. She showed me how strong and focused women can be. A fine role model, she had a concept called polarity therapy, which no one had ever heard of. Toning? Crystals? Energy? She built an empire of it and opened several schools. She is an author and is known as an "energy nerd," but she is mostly known for changing the lives of her students. Thank you, Nancy.

Chris Stecker

Chris introduced me to power of healing with sound. A group of students would lie on the carpet in a circle while Chris gently encircled us in a bath of sound from chakra bowls. The vibration in the room soared, and we were enveloped in healing. He taught me that masculine energy can be gentle and that not only women have the nurturing touch for healing. Thank you, Chris.

Trautle Weikman

Trautle enriched my life by bringing me deep within myself through the practice of body-centered meditation. I was the grasshopper, and she was the master. Trautle and I shared many private sessions as she taught me how to be comfortable while playing with authentic movement. It took years for me not to be embarrassed with grunting while dancing with authentic movement to drumming. The effect is very powerful. If I suggest authentic movement to you in the context of a session, and you are uneasy with it, I understand.

Bettina Zumdick

Meeting Bettina pulled all my prior knowledge into a concept that made sense. Bettina is a registered dietician and I quickly connected to her medical knowledge. Science, health, relationships, religion, or any topic presented by Bettina clarified my views and introduced me to new ones I had never considered. She made my life make sense. Her gentle manners made my harsh manners evident, which I still work on to this day. The way she holds her knife so gently with precision taught me the feminine aspects of being in your power. Her beauty radiates from deep within her, which is a quality I aspire to have. Her beautiful softness and loveliness are traits that reflect simply who she is. Sometimes I hear her voice as I am chopping vegetables or speaking at an event. I carry her spirit with me. She has been my teacher and mentor for more than twenty years, and every minute spent with her continues to build my understanding of this thing we call life. Her wisdom translates in the books she has written. There are no words to express my thanks.

Carrie Wolf

I remember Carrie telling me that there is no diet; there is only heavenly food. It took a long time for me to understand that. Carrie taught me not to take myself so seriously and that judgment and perfection are all in our minds. Thank you, Carrie.

Lucci Baranda

Lucci taught me that small women can hold a lot of power in their tiny bodies—the personal power with the mission to change life. Thank you, Lucci. RIP.

Charles Millman

Charles intrigued me from the moment I met him. His deep voice and tall structure infused his words into my understanding that the practice of macrobiotics is for everyone. Thank you, Charles.

John Kozinski

John's deep understanding of health filled the room as he spoke. I've listened to him lecture for hours without blinking because I wrote down every single word he ever said. I reflect on his teachings to this day. Thank you, John.

Diane Avoli

Diane lived macrobiotics to the fullest. She even harvested her own sea vegetables! Diane taught me that it didn't matter how inconvenient or time-consuming it is to cook at home. The reward is tenfold. She is right.

Edward Esko

When I think of Ed Esko, I hear the Beatles singing "Let it Be." He has whispered words of wisdom to me and those all around the world. His knowledge is astounding. His expertise shows in his playful personality. He holds the answers to many of our society's problems. Pick up one of his many books.

Alex Jack

A. J. is the backbone of our macrobiotic community. He has written many books, enlightened people around the globe, and taught me the many ways to see the same problem. It amazes me how strong a man can be by eating grain.

Abraham Oort

I met Abraham during a shiatzu class. He was the teacher—not just another strong man with kindness. I started to see a trend in macrobiotic men. He was the first person I saw who glowed. He actually had a light that emitted in and around him. The light in the room bounced off his skin. His flesh was clean and pure. After eating animals and sugar my whole life, he inspired me to clean my blood, raise my vibration, and glow! His words never taught me this; I learned simply from his radiance. I check the mirror every day to see how far I have come.

Mirea Ellis

Thank you, Mirea, for teaching me to dream. You brought my awareness to the deepest realms that I ever could imagine. Mirea also taught me to be a country girl. While learning the energetics of food, I told her that I really did not know which vegetables grew where. "I am a city girl," I said. "Aside from planting summer tomatoes as a kid, I do not understand what I am learning in class." That evening, after her shift was done, she took me foresting through the fields of the Kushi Institute. We were pulling up burdock root in the beautiful Berkshire mountains so I could see how it grows. I get it! Many thanks.

Shizuko Yamamoto

I had a shiatzu session once with Shizuko. A one-time meeting with her made a big impression on me. She stretched my arm beyond the point of pain, and when I expressed my discomfort, she emphatically stated, "Yin coming out," and it did. I cried for hours after that session for no apparent reason. I only knew that excess yin was coming out—most likely from the many bottles of soda I drank in high school.

Chris Jenkins

Chris is the most talented macrobiotic chef I've ever met. On the weekends at the Kushi Institute, Chris would make us some of his specialties. I'm salivating just remembering. Please write a cookbook, Chris, and thank you for inspiring me to serve my love in the food.

Toby Monte and Sherri Tenpenny

Toby and Sherri taught me the ugly truth about vaccines. I didn't learn that information in nursing school, and I will carry it with me always. I support your mission and think of you often. Thank you.

Tom Monte

My jaw hits the floor when I hear him speak. He combines macrobiotics with energy work and religion in a way that brings tears to my eyes. His message is one of beautiful truth. His passion for healing and the future of humanity comes through his teaching and books, and I will travel endless bounds to hear him speak. Tom has made a big impression on me. Thank you.

Marlene Watson Tara and Bill Tara

This inspiring couple embraces the mission of spreading veganism and health worldwide through their Human Ecology Project. I have read their many books and attended the classes that helped shape my life.

Christina Pirello

I bombarded Christina, who has written many books, with questions on how to start writing a book. "Do I use an outline? Where do I begin?

Do I organize my thoughts into chapters? Is there an app I can use?" She simply replied. "Just start writing." And I did.

None of this would ever be possible without the efforts of Michio Kushi, who brought macrobiotics to America from Japan with the purpose of creating peace. He was a leader in natural health with the vision of world peace through the practice of macrobiotics. A collection of his work can be seen at the Smithsonian Institute in Washington, DC. His vision on global peace earned him a nomination for a Nobel Peace Prize. My first meeting with Michio was interesting. He pointed to everyone in the classroom and said that it would take two years to learn the macrobiotic way. He then pointed to me and said, "You will take a lifetime." Here I am, thirty years later, writing my book. I think he was right.

References

(n.d.).

(2017). Retrieved from https://www.mountainhorsefarm.com/: https://www.mountainhorsefarm.com/.

(2020). Retrieved from Physicians Committee for Responsible Medicine: https://www.pcrm.org/.

(2020). Retrieved from safeSleeve: https://www.safesleevecases.com/.

A Call For Compassion Toward Animals. (2016). The Ant's Meow.

authors, 2. (2017). *The Bioinitiative 2012.* Retrieved from Bioinitiative Report: https://bioinitiative.org/

Campbell, T. (2005). Retrieved from The China Study-T.Colin Campbell Center for Nutrition Studies: https://nutritionstudies.org/the-china-study/.

Cao Jian Feng, Z. P. (2012). *Effect of aqueous extract of Arctium lappa L. (burdock) roots on the sexual behavior of male rats.* Retrieved from BMC Complementary Medicine and Therapies: https://www.ncbi.nlm.nih.gov/pmc/articles/PMC3299611/.

Chen, S. S. (2016). Plant Protease Inhibitors in Therapeutics—Focus on Cancer Therapy. *US National Library of Medicine National Institute of Health.*

Comprehensive Stool Analysis and Gut Flora Analysis. (2019). Retrieved from Verisana: https://www.verisana.com/gut-health-tests-1/comprehensive-stool-analysis-gut-flora-analysis.

Ecological burial pod turns bodies into trees. (2016, November 26). Retrieved from YouTube: https://www.youtube.com/watch?v=afc91CbdBzY.

Fiels, C. C.-R. (2018). *Effects of Gut-derived endotoxin on anxiety-like and repertitive behaviors in male ans female mice.* PubMed.gov.

FreelyGiveTruth2. (2013, August 28). *Seeds of Death: Unveiling the Lies of GMO's Full Documentary HD*. Retrieved from YouTube: https://www.youtube.com/watch?v=biQU9RnnGoM.
Group, E. W. (2005, July 14). *Body Burden: The Pollution in Newborns*. Retrieved from ewg: https://www.ewg.org/research/body-burden-pollution-newborns.
https://www.mountainhorsefarm.com/. (2017). *Mountain Horse Farm*.
Irradiated A comprehensive compilation of the literature on radiofrequency fields and the negative biological impacts of non-iodizing electromagnetic fields on biological organisms. (2017, April 10). Retrieved from Irradiated-FCC: https://ecfsapi.fcc.gov/file/1060927842647/irradiated.pdf.
Kushi, L. (2001). The Macrobiotic Diet in Cancer. *The Journal of Nutrition*. Retrieved from Macrobiotic Diet in Cancer-Oxford Academic Journals: https://academic.oup.com/jn/article/131/11/3056S/4686721.
Marcel Vogel Legacy. (n.d.).
mathieuasselin. (2013, November 16). *Monsanto vs. Farmers*. Retrieved from youTube: https://www.youtube.com/watch?v=GNvW-uGBTSk.
mcw. (2002). Are Microwave Ovens a Source of Danger? *The Journal of Natural Science*.
Medicine, P. C. (2019). *USDA Refuses to Protect Consumers From Fecal Contamination of Chicken and Other Meat*.
News, 1. A. (2018). *Salon Putting Live Ants Into Nails*.
Nine ways 5G and the internet of things will harm humans, wildlife, and earth. (2018). Retrieved from whatis5g.info: https://whatis5g.info.
Oppel, R. a. (2013). *Taping of Farm Cruelty is Becoming the Crime. New York Times*.
P.D.Darbre, A. A. (2004). Concentrations of Parabens in Human Breast Tumours. *Journal of Applied Toxicology*, 24, 5–13.
Patreon.com. (2017). *Why is 1.618034nso Important*. YouTube.
Press, A. (2017, March 15). *Yoga pants are destroying the Earth*. Retrieved from nypost.com: https://nypost.com/2017/03/15/yoga-pants-are-destroying-the-earth/.
R., E. (2016). *The Impossible Rice Experiment*.

Schelling, A. (2015). *Live Animals are Stuck Inside These Plastic Keychains.* the dodo.

Scientists link drinking milk with Osteoporosis. (2018, December 31). Retrieved from iphysio: https://iphysio.io/osteoporosis/.

Silverstone, A. (2011). Beans and Fartiness. A. Silverstone, *The Kind Diet: A Simple Guide to Feeling Great, Losing Weight, and Saving the Planet* (58).

Smart Meter Health Effects. (2020, February). Retrieved from emfanalysis: https://www.emfanalysis.com/smart-meter-health-effects/.

Society, G. (2016). 4 Myths About Food and Nutrition. *GI Socirty Canadian Society of Intestinal Research.*

Strombom, S. R. (2019). Colorectal Cancer Prevention With a Plant Based Diet. *Cancer Therapy and Oncology International Journal.*

Taketoshi Yoshida, K. M. (2018). *Association between cesarean section and constipation in infants: the Japanese Environment and children's study (JECS).* Retrieved from BMC Research Notes: https://bmcresnotes.biomedcentral.com/articles/10.1186/s13104-018-3990-5.

Webster, N. (ND). *Merriam-Webster Collegiate Dictionary.*

Wilson, L. (1995). *Soy Foods.* Retrieved from ScienceDirect: https://www.sciencedirect.com/topics/food-science/tempeh.

Yamamoto S, S. T. (2003). *Soy, isoflavones, and breast cancer risk in Japan.* Retrieved from Pubmed.gov: https://pubmed.ncbi.nlm.nih.gov/12813174/.

Yoshihiro Kokubo, M. H. (2007). Association of Dietary Intake of Soy Beans and Isoflavones with Risk of Cerebral and Myocardial Infarctions in Japanese Populations. *American Heart Association.*

Yuk-Shing Chan, L.-N. C.-H.-W.-Y.-H.-F.-W. (2011). *A Review of the Pharmacological Effects of ArctiumLappa (Burdock).* Retrieved from US National Library of Medicine: https://pubmed.ncbi.nlm.nih.gov/20981575/.

Index

Symbols

5G 260, 272

A

agar 217, 218, 229, 234, 235, 246
almond 96, 106, 115, 130, 195, 201, 202, 229, 232, 233, 237, 238, 240
    cream 50, 65, 72, 73, 112, 117, 203, 229, 232, 233, 235, 238
    miso almond sauce 195
amaranth 46, 71, 100, 101, 102, 103
    breakfast 31, 42, 43, 70, 86, 87, 88, 101, 102, 106, 162, 175
    popped 46, 100
    salad 47, 48, 83, 84, 85, 100, 103, 104, 105, 123, 124, 139, 150, 154, 156, 161, 166, 168, 169, 170, 171, 174, 192, 199, 205, 216, 217, 223
animal protein 12, 40, 45, 55, 56, 58, 66, 158, 244
apple 59, 83, 84, 132, 144, 146, 156, 165, 169, 188, 192, 199, 203, 219, 222, 229, 232, 235, 236, 239
    fruit crumble 236
    A is for apple (baked) 239
    undressed pressed salad 169
    warm barley salad 83, 84
arame 218, 222, 223
    mermaid salad 223
    the need for weed 222
avocado 71, 109, 117, 149, 165, 198, 203, 221
    avocado salado 198
    A chick's sandwich 149
    silly Lily's chili 116, 118
    the whole bowl 109, 110
awn 37

B

barley 41, 44, 45, 61, 62, 80, 82, 83, 84, 240
    barley three ways 82
    lauren's lentil love 142
    roomy rice 80, 81
    warm barley salad 83, 84
beans xxii, 61, 71, 109, 111, 117, 136, 139, 140, 144, 145, 146, 148, 150, 151, 159, 179, 216, 218, 241, 242, 245, 273
    adzuki beans and sweet rice 151
    clean bean salad 150
    there's a bean in my truffle 241, 242

skinny jeans lima beans 144, 145
a bowl of escarole 136
can't beat this meat 146, 147
A chick's sandwich 149
chicky peas 148
tofu feta is betta 154
Lauren's lentil love 142
magazine navy beans 159
more cheese please 155
red lentils 141
scrambled tofu 152
silly Lily's Chili 116, 118
tempeh and cabbage 156, 157
the whole bowl 109, 110
blood quality 119, 162, 220, 224, 243, 244, 245, 264
breath 1, 3, 11, 14, 16, 18, 19, 67, 248, 249, 250, 251, 252, 253
breathe vii, xvii, 3, 7, 11, 14, 16, 18, 23, 49, 70, 248, 249, 250, 251, 252, 253, 263
brine 210, 211
brown rice viii, 12, 35, 36, 38, 39, 44, 71, 72, 73, 74, 75, 76, 77, 78, 80, 85, 88, 89, 104, 106, 109, 113, 115, 138, 151, 152, 183, 188, 189, 190, 193, 201, 202, 203, 204, 205, 207, 219, 221, 222, 223, 227, 229, 232, 233, 234, 235, 237, 238, 247
  azuki beans and sweet rice 151
  baby dreams of rice cream 72
  boiled brown rice 76
  classic brown rice morning porridge 88
  the need for weed (seaweed with rice) 222
  nice fried rice 76, 77
  rice by the pound 238
  pressure-cooked rice 74
  rice balls 78
  rice is my vice salad 85
  roomy rice 80, 81
  snap, crackle, and crunch treats, 237
  the story of nori 221
  the whole bowl 109, 110
brown rice syrup 73, 106, 113, 115, 138, 183, 193, 203, 204, 219, 227, 229, 233, 234, 235, 237, 238, 247
buckwheat 47, 71, 80, 86, 107, 108, 123
  breakfast porridge 86, 87
  buckwheat bread instead 108
  buckwheat noodles 123
  bucky-wheat and greens 107
  roomy rice 80, 81
bulgur wheat 84, 116, 172
burdock root 120, 185, 186, 268
  gentle lentil soup 120
  in cahoots with roots 185
  kinpira with lotus root 186
burial pod 262, 271

C

C-8 261
carrot tops 178
cauliflower 90, 109, 134, 162, 165, 166, 190, 191, 206, 211
  all over leftover soup 134
  I will shoyu pickles 211
  mashed millet 90, 91
  my own biome pickles 206, 208
  the power of cauliflower 190, 191
  the royal boil salad 166
  the whole bowl 109, 110
chakra xi, xii, xvi, xvii, xxii, 2, 4, 5, 6, 7, 8, 9, 10, 11, 13, 14, 15, 16, 17, 18, 19, 20, 21, 22, 23, 24, 25, 27, 29, 33, 34, 38, 45,

57, 68, 77, 114, 243, 250, 251, 252, 253, 254, 259, 265
cheese 50, 65, 113, 154, 155
    tofu feta is betta 154
    more cheese please 155
chestnut 234, 238
    chestnut puree 234
    rice by the pound 238
chickpeas 148, 149
    A chick's sandwich 149
    chicky peas 148
chili 116, 117, 118
    silly Lily's chili 116, 118
chowder 130, 131
    corny chowder 130, 131
corn 41, 46, 47, 48, 58, 59, 79, 84, 85, 101, 102, 109, 112, 115, 117, 130, 141, 144, 145, 150, 165, 219, 220, 224, 243, 258
    clean bean salad 150
    skinny jeans lima beans 144, 145
    breakfast amaranth 101, 102
    corny chowder 130, 131
    don't dread my cornbread 115, 118
    patty cake 112
    red lentils 141
    rice is my vice salad 85
    silly Lily's chili 116, 118
    treasures at sea 219, 220
    warm barley salad 83, 84
    the whole bowl 109, 110
cornbread 115, 118
    don't dread my cornbread 115, 118
cream 50, 65, 72, 73, 112, 117, 203, 229, 232, 233, 235, 238
    almond cream 229, 233, 238
    chestnut puree 234
    creamy dreamy dressing 202
    happy day parfait 229, 230, 232

    lemon Kanten 235
    Kayla loves cashew cream 232
    patty cake 112
    rice by the pound 238
    silly Lily's chili 116, 118
crumble 152, 236
    fruit crumble 236
crystals xvii, xix, 10, 22, 23, 24, 25, 26, 27, 168, 265

D

daikon 162, 166, 171, 181, 183, 184, 221
    hail to kale 171
    mimi's nishimi 181
    the royal boil salad 166
    the story of nori 221
    tic-tac daikon 183
dressing 63, 82, 85, 104, 107, 109, 164, 166, 167, 169, 171, 190, 192, 193, 194, 196, 197, 199, 200, 201, 202, 203, 205, 223
    ballard dressing 104
    bellini tahini dressing 197
    bucky-wheat and greens 107
    the creamy almond 201
    creamy dreamy dressing 202
    Donna's famous salad dressing 192
    dreamy tahini sauce 201
    no messing with this dressing 200
    the power of cauliflower 190, 191
    pumpkin seed dressing 164, 166, 167, 196
    supreme sour cream 112, 117, 203
    trick or treat beet dressing 205
    vampire's dressing 199
    very strawberry dressing 199
dulse 217

E

escarole 136, 137
    a bowl of escarole 136

F

farro 46, 71, 104, 105
    the ballad of farro salad 104

G

gluten 44, 45, 46, 47, 48, 58, 113, 115, 123, 218
GMO 34, 102, 258, 259, 272
grain viii, xi, xiii, xx, xxii, xxiii, xxiv, 12, 34, 35, 36, 37, 38, 39, 40, 41, 42, 43, 44, 45, 46, 47, 48, 52, 54, 57, 60, 61, 64, 65, 66, 67, 68, 70, 71, 72, 73, 74, 76, 77, 78, 79, 80, 84, 85, 86, 88, 99, 109, 112, 117, 134, 139, 140, 142, 156, 158, 180, 195, 201, 216, 217, 221, 222, 225, 227, 245, 247, 253, 255, 258, 263, 264, 268
    all over leftover soup 134
    baby dreams of rice cream 72
    the ballad of farro salad 104
    barley three ways 82
    boiled brown rice 76
    breakfast amaranth 101, 102
    breakfast porridge 86, 87
    buckwheat bread instead 108
    bucky-wheat and greens 107
    classic brown rice morning porridge 88
    don't dread my corn bread 115
    fill it with millet 98
    grain cooking chart 71
    Lauren's lentil love 142
    mashed millet 90, 91
    millet with sweet vegetables 93
    mochi puffs 113
    the need for weed (seaweed with rice) 222
    nice fried rice 76, 77
    paradise rice 114
    patty cake 112
    A-hint-a polenta 111
    popped amaranth 100
    pressure-cooked rice 74
    queen of quinoa 94, 95
    rah rah quinoa 99
    rice balls 78
    rice is my vice salad 85
    the romance of amaranth (salad) 103
    roomy rice 80, 81
    the story of nori 221
    tempeh and cabbage 156, 157
    tote your oats 106
    warm barley salad 83, 84
    the whole bowl 109, 110
    winner takes all millet balls 96, 98
gravy 90, 91, 92, 179
    mashed millet 90, 91
    mushroom gravy 90, 91, 92
greens 14, 42, 47, 55, 80, 84, 94, 98, 104, 107, 109, 113, 114, 117, 120, 122, 128, 134, 161, 162, 164, 166, 167, 168, 169, 171, 172, 175, 177, 178, 188, 206, 211, 215, 218, 222, 223, 236, 262
    all over leftover soup 134
    the ballad of farro salad 104
    bitatho 172, 173
    boasted roasted vegetables 179
    bucky-wheat and greens 107
    fill it with millet 98
    flip-flops and carrot tops 178
    hail to kale 171

high on stir fry 188, 189
hump day greens 172
my own biome pickles 206, 208
paradise rice 114
the power of cauliflower 190, 191
roomy rice 80, 81
the royal boil salad 166
sauerkraut 63, 164, 209, 222
steamed greens with envy 175
undressed pressed salad 169
soba up 122
warm barley salad 83, 84
the whole bowl 109, 110
who stole my roll 164
gut 15, 33, 40, 57, 58, 59, 60, 61, 63, 66, 79, 116, 128, 139, 140, 209, 211, 231, 243, 246, 247, 258, 271

H

hijiki 209, 215, 216, 218, 219
sauerkraut 63, 164, 209, 222
treasures at sea 219, 220
honeydew 138, 165
deja vu honeydew 138

K

kale 104, 107, 109, 122, 128, 134, 165, 166, 171, 172, 175, 176
all over left over soup 134
the ballad of farro salad 104
bucky-wheat and greens 107
hail to kale 171
hump day greens 172
me so healthy miso soup 128
the royal boil salad 166
steamed greens with envy 175
soba up 122
the whole bowl 109, 110
kanten 234, 235
kinpira 185, 186

kombu 70, 73, 74, 76, 80, 88, 93, 94, 114, 122, 125, 126, 127, 128, 140, 142, 144, 148, 151, 159, 181, 216, 217, 218, 222, 241
azuki beans and sweet rice 151
there's a bean in my truffle 241, 242
skinny jeans lima beans 144, 145
boiled brown rice 76
chicky peas 148
classic brown rice morning porridge 88
kombu broth 122, 125, 126, 127, 128
Lauren's lentil love 142
magazine navy beans 159
me so healthy miso soup 128
millet with sweet vegetables 93
mimi's nishimi 181
the need for weed (seaweed with rice) 222
paradise rice 114
pressure cooked rice 74
queen of quinoa 94, 95
roomy rice 80, 81
soba up 122
whiskey tofu soup 127
kudzu 92, 127, 188, 195, 229, 231, 236
the boss of sauce 195
fruit crumble 236
happy day parfait 229, 230, 232
high on stir fry 188, 189
mushroom gravy 90, 91, 92
whiskey tofu soup 127
kuzu 231

L

lemon walnut dunk 204
lentil 94, 109, 120, 121, 139, 141, 142, 143

gentle lentil soup 120
Lauren's lentil love 142
queen of quinoa 94, 95
red lentils 141
the whole bowl 109, 110
lentils 94, 109, 120, 121, 139, 141, 142, 143
Life force 1, 2, 4, 9, 16, 20, 21, 23, 28, 29, 30, 34, 36, 39, 47, 65, 160, 224, 225, 243, 249, 251, 259, 260

M

meat xvi, xxi, xxii, 36, 40, 41, 45, 48, 49, 51, 52, 54, 55, 56, 66, 139, 146, 147, 272
meridians xxii, 29, 30, 31, 32, 45, 64, 161, 253, 254, 260
microbiome 57, 60, 61, 66
millet 41, 44, 71, 84, 90, 91, 93, 96, 97, 98, 111, 152
    fill it with millet 98
    mashed millet 90, 91
    millet with sweet vegetables 93
    A-hint-a polenta 111
    scrambled tofu 152
    winner takes all millet balls 96
minerals 36, 66, 119, 157, 212, 213, 215, 216, 217, 218, 224, 225, 226, 243, 246
miso 42, 61, 62, 63, 82, 86, 104, 120, 128, 129, 130, 134, 136, 142, 144, 145, 148, 155, 159, 168, 183, 184, 195, 198, 201, 207, 216, 233, 237, 239
    all over leftover soup 134
    almond cream 229, 233, 238
    avocado salado 198
    ballard dressing 104
    barley three ways 82
    skinny jeans lima bean 144, 145
    a bowl of escarole 136
    breakfast porridge 86, 87
    chicky peas 148
    corny chowder 130, 131
    dreamy tahini sauce 201
    gentle lentil soup 120
    A is for apple 239
    Lauren's lentil love 142
    magazine navy beans 159
    me so healthy miso soup 128
    miso almond sauce 195
    more cheese please 155
    my own biome pickles 206, 208
    snap, crackle, and crunch treats 237
    tic-tac-daikon 183
mochi 36, 98, 113, 179
    boasted roasted vegetables 179
    fill it with millet 98
    mochi puffs 113
molo 240

N

nishimi 181, 182
nori 43, 78, 106, 217, 221
    rice balls 78
    the story of nori 221
    tote your oats 106

O

oats 41, 46, 84, 86, 106, 158
    breakfast porridge 86, 87
    tote your oats 106
onion jam 180

P

paraben 255, 256, 272
parfait 229, 230, 232
patty cake 112
physiognomy 64

pickles 42, 63, 109, 149, 169, 170, 171, 206, 208, 211, 222
    I will shoyu pickles 211
    my own biome pickles 206, 208
    the story of nori 221
    the whole bowl 109, 110
polenta 48, 111, 112, 115, 130, 152
    corny chowder 130, 131
    don't dread my cornbread 115
    patty cake 112
    A-hint-a polenta 111
    scrambled tofu 152
porridge 42, 43, 46, 70, 86, 87, 88, 89
    breakfast porridge 86, 87
    classic brown rice morning porridge 88

Q

quinoa 45, 47, 71, 84, 94, 95, 99, 109, 112, 116
    a warm barley salad 83
    patty cake 112
    queen of quinoa 94, 95
    rah rah quinoa 99
    silly Lily's chili 116, 118
    the whole bowl 109, 110

R

radiation 215, 259, 260
rice viii, xiii, xiv, xxiii, xxiv, 3, 12, 34, 35, 36, 37, 38, 39, 41, 44, 46, 53, 56, 61, 71, 72, 73, 74, 75, 76, 77, 78, 80, 81, 83, 84, 85, 88, 89, 104, 106, 109, 113, 114, 115, 125, 138, 151, 152, 174, 183, 188, 189, 190, 192, 193, 199, 201, 202, 203, 204, 205, 207, 219, 221, 222, 223, 227, 229, 232, 233, 234, 235, 237, 238, 246, 247, 262, 263, 272
    azuki beans and sweet rice 151
    baby dream of rice cream 72
    boiled brown rice 76
    classic brown rice morning porridge 88
    high on stir fry 188, 189
    the need for weed (seaweed with rice) 222
    nice fried rice 76, 77
    paradise rice 114
    rice by the pound 238
    pressure-cooked rice 74
    rice balls 78
    rice is my vice salad 85
    roomy rice 80, 81
    scrambled tofu 152
    snap, crackle, and crunch treats 237
    the story of nori 221
    warm barley salad 83, 84
    the whole bowl 109, 110
rutabaga 86, 120, 148, 181, 211
    breakfast porridge 86, 87
    chicky peas 148
    gentle lentil soup 120
    I will shoyu pickles 211
    mimi's nishimi 181

S

salad 47, 48, 83, 84, 85, 100, 103, 104, 105, 123, 124, 139, 150, 154, 156, 161, 166, 168, 169, 170, 171, 174, 192, 199, 205, 216, 217, 223
    avocado salado 198
    the ballad of farro salad 104
    clean bean salad 150
    hail to kale 171
    mermaid salad 223

soba noodle salad 124
popped amaranth 100
rice is my vice salad 85
the romance of amaranth
    (salad) 103
the royal boil salad 166
soba soup 123
tofu feta is betta 154
undressed pressed salad 169
warm barley salad 83, 84
zero point cucumber salad 174
sauce 113, 117, 164, 179, 188, 195,
    201, 205, 221
    the boss of sauce 195
    dreamy tahini sauce 201
    trick or treat beet dressing 205
sauerkraut 63, 164, 209, 222
    the story of nori 221
    who stole my roll 164
seaweed 215, 217, 221, 222
sesame seeds 108, 178, 185, 190, 218,
    219, 220, 223, 227, 238
    buckwheat bread instead 108
    flip-flops and carrot tops 178
    in cahoots with roots 185
    mermaid salad 223
    rice by the pound 238
    the power of cauliflower 190, 191
    bars for the stars 227, 228
    treasures at sea 219, 220
shoyu 63, 77, 92, 96, 103, 107, 122,
    146, 156, 168, 178, 179, 181,
    183, 185, 188, 195, 199, 211,
    222, 223, 224, 225
    boasted roasted vegetables 179
    the boss of sauce 195
    bucky-wheat and greens 107
    can't beat this meat 146, 147
    flip-flops and carrot tops 178
    high on stir fry 188, 189
    in cahoots with roots 185

I will shoyu pickles 211
mermaid salad 223
mimi's nishimi 181
mushroom gravy 90, 91, 92
the need for weed (seaweed with
    rice) 222
nice fried rice 76, 77
the romance of amaranth
    (salad) 103
tempeh and cabbage 156, 157
tic-tac-daikon 183
soba up 122
very strawberry dressing 199
winner takes all millet balls
    96, 98
soba 47, 122, 123, 124, 195
    miso almond sauce 195
    soba noodle salad 124
    soba soup 123
    soba up 122
soup 42, 43, 51, 63, 82, 106, 116,
    120, 122, 123, 125, 127, 128,
    129, 130, 132, 133, 134, 135,
    136, 138, 141, 148, 160, 216
    all over leftover soup 134
    a bowl of escarole 136
    corny chowder 130, 131
    deja vu honeydew 138
    gentle lentil soup 120
    kombu broth 122, 125, 126,
        127, 128
    me so healthy miso soup 128
    silly Lily's chili 116, 118
    soba soup 123
    sweet autumn harvest soup
        132, 133
    whiskey tofu soup 127
sour cream 112, 117, 203
stir fry 82, 123, 188, 189
sugar xvi, 8, 12, 14, 15, 35, 45, 58,
    59, 60, 61, 63, 65, 66, 67, 69,

93, 102, 174, 217, 218, 225, 231, 240, 242, 243, 244, 245, 246, 247, 258, 268

T

tempeh 63, 77, 109, 146, 152, 156, 157, 158, 222, 273
- can't beat this meat 146, 147
- the whole bowl 109, 110

tofu 54, 77, 109, 127, 128, 152, 153, 154, 155, 195, 200, 203, 218, 222
- tofu feta is betta 154
- me so healthy miso soup 128
- more cheese please 155
- scrambled tofu 152
- supreme sour cream 112, 117, 203
- whiskey tofu soup 127
- the whole bowl 109, 110

treats 78, 205, 217, 227, 237, 247
- fruit crumble 236
- happy day parfait 229, 230, 232
- lemon kanten 235
- rice balls 78
- snap, crackle, and crunch treats, 237
- bars for the stars 227, 228
- there's a bean in my truffle 241, 242

truffle 241, 242

U

umeboshi 63, 78, 79, 88, 150, 154, 168, 175, 190, 196, 200, 203, 221
- clean bean salad 150
- classic brown rice morning porridge 88
- tofu feta is betta 154
- no messing with this dressing 200
- the power of cauliflower 190, 191
- pumpkin seed dressing 164, 166, 167, 196
- rice balls 78
- steamed greens with envy 175
- the story of nori 221
- supreme sour cream 112, 117, 203

W

wakame 103, 128, 174, 216, 217
- me so healthy miso soup 128
- the romance of amaranth (salad) 103
- zero point cucumber salad 174

whole bowl 109, 110

Printed in Great Britain
by Amazon